2/97

JL

WITHDRAWN

Women of Valor

STORIES OF GREAT JEWISH WOMEN
WHO HELPED SHAPE THE TWENTIETH CENTURY

Women of Valor

STORIES OF GREAT JEWISH WOMEN
WHO HELPED SHAPE THE TWENTIETH CENTURY

Sheila Segal

Foreword by Gloria Goldreich

BEHRMAN HOUSE, INC.

DEDICATION

For Danny, who is with me in everything I do

—S.S.

Copyright © 1996 by Sheila Segal

The author and publisher gratefully acknowledge the following sources of photographs for this book:

The author and publisher gratefully acknowledge the following sources of photographs for this book: Robert F. Wagner Labor Archives, New York University, Rose Schneiderman Collection: 1, 5, 17; The Jewish Museum/Art Resource, NY: 3; Museum of the City of New York: The Byron Collection: 7; ILGWU Archives, The Kheel Documentation Center, Cornell University: 10; Amalgamated Clothing and Textile Workers Union: 13; Brown Brothers: 14 (top and bottom); courtesy of Hadassah, the Women's Zionist Organization of America: 19, 21, 23; Central Zionist Archive, Jerusalem: 26, 30, 31, 64; Leo Baeck Institute: 29; Israel Goverment Press Office: 34; Library of Congress: 36; Yad Vashem, Jerusalem: 39; 42, 43, 48; YIVO Institute for Jewish Research: 57; UPI/Corbis-Bettman: 45, 58, 74, 78, 92, 125; National Archives: 50; Georgia and Steven Solotoff: 51; Jerry Bergman: 52; Museum of the City of New York: The Theatre Collection: 55, 60, 61, 62; courtesy of Ida Nudel: 66, 80; Reuters/ Dominique Dudouble/ Archive Photos: 71; Bill Aron Photography: 73; Reuters/Corbis-Bettman: 77, 88, 89, 119, 126, 127; UJA Press Service/ Richard Lobell: 81; courtesy of Julia Partners: 83; courtesy of Shoshana Cardin: 85, 96, 99; Corbis Bettman: 87 (top); David Karp: 87 (inset); Reuters/UPI/Corbis-Bettman: 95; Isaac Freidin: 101; Amit Women: 105; David Rubinger: 111; Courtesy of Yael Arad: 115; Archive/Reuters/ K. Mayama: 127; Fraser Communications: 127 (inset), 128; Maccabi USA Sports for Israel/The Israel Olympic Committee: 120, 124.

The author and publisher would like to thank Ida Nudel, Shoshana Cardin, and Yael Arad for graciously providing photographs from their personal collections.

Library of Congress Cataloging-in-Publication Data

Segal, Sheila F.
   Women of Valor: stories of great Jewish women who helped shape the twentieth century/Sheila Segal.
144 p. cm.
   Summary: Biographies of eight women who made unique contributions of Jewish life, including union organizer Rose Schneiderman, founder of Hadassah Henrietta Szold, and Israel's first Olympic medalist Yael Arad.
   ISBN 0-087441-612-4
   1. Jewish women—Biography—Juvenile literature. [1. Jews—Biography. 2. Women Biography.]
I. Title.
DS115.2.S44 1996
920.72'089'924—dc20
[B]
          96-28372
          CIP
          AC

Printed in the United States of America

10 9 8 7 6 5 4 3 2

Published by Behrman House, Inc.
235 Watchung Avenue
West Orange, NJ 07052

ISBN: 0-87441-612-4

Editor: Sarah Feldman
Book Design: Howard Levy Design

Contents

Foreword

The eight Jewish women who spring to life on the pages of this important book confronted the challenges of the twentieth century with courage and tenacity. In an era of social and technological revolution, horrendous wars, and uneasy peace, these women laid claim to the values of the Jewish tradition and used these values to make the world a better and safer place to live.

During the years of their lives, the course of Jewish history was altered forever, first by the great immigration from eastern Europe to the United States, then by the terror of the Holocaust, and finally by the glorious birth of the State of Israel. These historic events impacted on the lives of these women who dared to seize the day, to respond with creativity and energy to the needs of their people and thus to guarantee an enriched and enlightened future.

From Rose Schneiderman, an immigrant sweat shop worker who sought social justice in the nascent labor movement, to Henrietta Szold, initiator and organizer of the movement that rescued Jewish children from Nazi-occupied Europe, to Yael Arad, Israel's first Olympic medalist, who dedicated her triumph to her murdered fellow athletes, each woman in this book made a unique contribution to the course of world history by embracing a commitment to an ideal and working to translate that ideal into an enduring reality.

Neither a need for fame nor a desire for power motivated them; they wanted recognition for their causes, not for themselves. Indeed, fame eluded many of them, and while their achievements endure, their names are in danger of receding into history.

We are grateful then, for this exciting chronicle. For we meet these women as individuals, whose backgrounds are familiar to us—sisters and daughters, loving friends, they struggled with doubt and uncertainty, overcame personal hardships yet never lost sight of their goals. They came from different parts of the world and lived at different times of the century, yet all proved the power that can be generated when dreams are fired by determination. They are proof that Jewish women play an important role in molding today's world and in forging the way for a new generation poised on the cusp of a new century.

—GLORIA GOLDREICH

Introduction

*R*aise the subject of great Jewish women, and one name comes to mind: Golda Meir. Everyone, it seems, knows Golda. After all, she is the only woman to have served as prime minister of Israel, thus culminating a lifetime devoted to building the Jewish state. It is no wonder hers is the first name on everybody's list.

What is surprising, however, is that the list usually ends there. Some people manage to come up with another name or two: usually that of Hannah Senesh, the Haganah fighter who parachuted to her death on an extraordinary rescue mission in Nazi-occupied Europe; or Anne Frank, whose diary of her early teen years in hiding from the Nazis is a testament to the human spirit. And some people mention Jewish women whose accomplishments have been in the general community, such as television journalist Barbara Walters or U.S. Supreme Court Justice Ruth Bader Ginsburg. But when it comes to women who have had a great impact on Jewish life, few names surface other than Golda Meir.

Of course, there's no one like Golda Meir. And there is no one like Hannah Senesh or Anne Frank, either. We are fortunate that their inspiring stories are widely available in books for young people and adults. But the twentieth century has produced many other Jewish women who have made unique contributions to Jewish life. They are women of great courage and accomplishment whose names are too easily forgotten and whose stories are rarely told.

In Jewish history, as in general history, the public accomplishments of individual women have usually been ignored or glossed over. When a woman's activities outside the family do earn her some attention, she is often portrayed as so exceptional that she could not possibly be a role model for other women. Or she is treated as an eccentric whose behavior is contrary to true female nature, as when David Ben-Gurion, Israel's first prime minister, described Golda Meir as "the only man in my cabinet."

Golda may indeed have been tougher and shrewder than the men around her. But is it really unwomanly to act out of deep commitment, to be totally devoted to a cause, or to want to shape a better future? Is it unnatural for a woman to fight for what she believes is important and, like Golda, to have the strength to tough it out?

Women of achievement go about things differently than do men, and this is another reason why these women have received so little recognition in our history books. Power seems to interest them less than principle. They are more concerned with tackling the problems they see than with calling attention to their own roles in solving them. Even where credit is clearly due, women often seem reluctant to claim it for themselves.

As a result, we sometimes have to look extra hard to see the significant roles that women have played outside their families. When we make that effort, however, we find a surprising number of women who have truly made a difference—not only as daughters, wives, and mothers but also as leaders, thinkers, and fighters. We also see that they have done so not by trying to be like men but by having the courage to be themselves.

This book focuses on eight such women. They are women whose accomplishments span the twentieth century and impact many areas of Jewish life. Their stories demonstrate the creativity and strength of women at different stages in the life cycle, from their teens to their eighties. And they provide us with personal experiences of the most important aspects of Jewish history in our century: Jewish trade unionism on the Lower East Side, the Zionist movement in America and Europe, the resettlement of Palestine and the birth of Israel, the Holocaust, Jewish life under Communism, the organized American Jewish community, and the world of Torah study.

I have selected only eight individuals for this volume, though many other women could have been included. It is my hope that by limiting the number, and spending more time with each woman, we will come to understand not only their goals, strategies, and accomplishments but also their fears, conflicts, and uncertainties. As we get to know what makes these women tick and how they tackle the challenges before them, these "women of valor" become more than exceptional cases who inspire our awe. We see that they are real people after all, and as real people they can truly be models for our own lives.

— SHEILA SEGAL

CHAPTER 1

Rose Schneiderman
VOICE OF A FACTORY GIRL
(1882–1972)

*B*orn in eastern Poland in 1882, Rose Schneiderman *was eight years old when her family set out for America, the land of opportunity. Like hundreds of thousands of Jewish immigrants near the turn of the century, the Schneidermans came to New York's Lower East Side. But instead of the fabled "streets paved with gold," they found filth, poverty, hunger, and unemployment. The lucky ones found jobs in the sweat*

*shops of the garment industry, where they worked for meager
wages under appalling conditions.*

*As the new century got under way, a radical movement
called "trade unionism" began to spread the idea that poor
workers could do something about their plight if they banded
together and spoke out as one. Rose Schneiderman was one of
those who awoke to the call. She threw herself into the trade
union movement and inspired countless women to join her in
the struggle for a better life. When a preventable factory fire
killed scores of female workers, Rose Schneiderman sounded a
cry of protest that would no longer go unheeded.*

*R*ose Schneiderman turned away from the mirror and looked
around at the shabby tenement where her family lived—no electricity,
gas, or running water; five people crowded into two tiny rooms.
How could she bring friends home to visit when there wasn't an
inch of private space, a comfortable place to sit, or an extra dime for
refreshments? She wouldn't be seeing her friends at school either
now that she was going out to work.

For Rose Schneiderman, as for many poor immigrant girls on the
Lower East Side, life was a lonely and dreary affair. There was no
money for anything extra—like going out for an ice-cream soda or
buying a book. A girl was lucky if she even got to go to school, luckier
still if she could finish elementary school. But if her family was
struggling to get by, as the Schneidermans were, then coming of age
meant going out to work to help support the household.

This was not the life Sam Schneiderman had in mind for his
daughter. He had come to America so that his children would have
the education and the opportunities he had never had. Then, in the
winter of 1892, the future was snatched away from him. One night
Sam Schneiderman returned from his factory job burning with
fever. Three days later he was dead, struck down by an influenza
epidemic that was spreading uncontrollably through the dirty and

crowded neighborhoods of the Lower East Side. Sam left his wife, Devora, who spoke no English, three young children, and a baby due any day.

For Rose, who always had a special relationship with her father, his death was a terrible blow. At a time when most parents thought it more important to educate their sons than their daughters, Sam had encouraged his daughter's interest in reading and urged her to study hard in school. He was going to make sure she could pursue her dream of becoming a teacher. Now, with her father gone, all that seemed impossible. Rose couldn't even imagine how her family would survive.

The family did survive, but only through the kindness of United Hebrew Charities, which sent food regularly until the baby was born and Devora was strong enough to take in some sewing. A few months later Devora took a full-time job in a factory, sewing linings into fur capes. The hours were long and the wages were low, but at least the paycheck was steady. The catch was that Rose, who was only ten years old, would have to stay home with her baby sister, Jane; and her younger brothers, Charlie and Harry, would have to go to an orphanage. It was the only way the Schneidermans could get by.

The Lower East Side on a typical business day in 1912. This crowded neighborhood was the first home for many immigrants who arrived in New York from eastern Europe.

More than a year passed before Rose could return to school. She caught up quickly, moved beyond her age level, and revived her dreams of becoming a teacher. But when Devora suddenly lost her job at the factory, Rose had to withdraw from school again. Now it was her turn to go out and work. At the age of thirteen, she was about to become the family's breadwinner.

For Women Only

What kind of work was there for a young immigrant girl without much education? At the turn of the century, the number of female workers in the United States was rising steadily, especially in the poor immigrant communities. The options, however, were very limited.

For the greenhorns—immigrants who knew little or no English—factory jobs were the easiest to come by: You didn't have to know English to slave all day at a sewing machine. But for those who spoke English, there were more desirable possibilities, such as working as a salesclerk in one of the big, new department stores. Most enviable was a job as a typist or a clerk in an office, where the chances of finding an educated husband were best. The idea that a young woman might work to satisfy a personal interest or to gain independence was almost unheard of.

Rose had no special skills, but her English and math were good enough to land her a job at Hearn's Department Store, at a salary of $2.16 for a sixty-four-hour week. Three years later Rose was still working in a department store, earning $2.75 a week and growing very impatient. She began to think about making a switch—going to one of the factories, where workers could earn a great deal more. Devora did not want her daughter working in one of those awful places even if the salary was higher. For Rose, however, it was a simple economic issue: She wanted to rise above poverty.

With the pennies she had been saving each week, Rose bought a secondhand sewing machine for thirty dollars. She quickly learned how to use it and found a job with Fox & Lederer, a cap factory, starting at about twice her former salary. At last her family could breathe more easily, but Rose now understood why women preferred to stay away from factories.

At Fox & Lederer the male workers cut and sewed the caps

while the female workers made the linings. Lining makers had to provide their own sewing machines, thread, and any other supplies they needed. The factory owners didn't care that these expenses cut into their workers' earnings. Nor did they care about the ill effects of the airless and overcrowded workrooms or the long hours that the

men and women spent hunched over their machines. They cared only about their profits, and that meant producing their goods as cheaply and as quickly as possible.

Six days a week, ten hours a day, Rose Schneiderman endured the drudgery and injustice of her situation. With no money to spare and no time or energy to spend on any other activities, she escaped into the world of romantic novels, novels filled with intelligent and idealistic characters who were unlike anyone in her own world—that is, until she met Bessie Braut.

Rose Schneiderman at her sewing machine. Many women were forced to work in sweatshops where they sat bent over their work for twelve to eighteen hours a day.

Bessie Braut came to Fox & Lederer early in 1923 and told her co-workers, most of them recent Jewish immigrants, that they didn't have to tolerate inhumane working conditions. She explained that workers all over the United States were joining together and forming trade unions in order to express their grievances. Together, she said, workers had the power to improve their lives and create a more just society.

The trade union movement was already attracting many Jewish workers on the Lower East Side, but until Bessie Braut came on the scene, the young women at Fox & Lederer knew almost nothing about it. They had no idea that there was a union in their own industry. They were even more surprised to hear that women could join, too. Even though women comprised more than 70 percent of the labor force in the garment industry, there had been no active effort to bring them into the union membership.

Rose Schneiderman and Bessie Braut set out to change that. Along with another co-worker, Bessie Mannis, they became a committee to look into forming a local union chapter for female cap makers. Together the three women went to the New York headquarters of the United Cloth Hat and Cap Makers Union to put forward their request. All they had to do, the secretary explained, was recruit twenty-five female cap makers and present their names and signatures. How hard could that be?

There was only one way to find out. That same day, at closing time, the three women went out and stationed themselves at factory doors. With blank membership forms in hand, they were ready to talk with the women who emerged. Many were afraid to get involved with the unions, afraid of angering their employers and losing their jobs. Nevertheless, within three days Schneiderman, Braut, and Mannis had the signatures they needed.

In January 1903, the new union was officially chartered as Local 23 of the International Ladies' Garment Workers' Union (ILGWU), an organization that included many types of workers involved in the production of ladies' clothing. The ILGWU and its local chapters were known as the "Jewish unions" because the largest percentage of their members were Jews. Local 23 was the first union of female workers—not only among the Jewish unions but in the entire garment industry. Its first order of business was to elect a secretary—twenty-one-year-old Rose Schneiderman.

To Lillian Wald, a Jewish nurse who had been living and working on the Lower East Side since the early 1880s, it was truly inspiring to see what this "poor young cap maker" was able to accomplish. "Despite her long hours," Wald wrote in her memoirs, "she found time to organize a union in her trade, not in a spurt of enthusiasm, but as a result of a sober realization that women workers must stand together for themselves and for those who come after them."

A Shared Ideal

Lillian Wald, raised in a well-to-do family of German Jews, was one of many women who were not part of the working class but were dedicated to helping their less fortunate sisters. In 1903, the same year that Local 23 was born, a group of those women founded a national organization called the Women's Trade Union League (WTUL). Its goal was to encourage women to join the trade union movement and to help women organize against the dangers and injustices of the workplace.

Rose Schneiderman heard about the WTUL in 1904, and she soon became involved in its New York chapter. By 1906 she was vice president. In the meantime she had become a member of the executive board of the ILGWU, the first woman elected to a leadership position in the trade union movement. And she was still the secretary of Local 23, the female cap makers. Her lonely and unhappy life was now filled with wonderful new friends and devoted to a great ideal that they all shared.

Devora Schneiderman, however, was not at all happy about her daughter's participation in trade unionism. She worried that it would ruin her chances for marriage and a family. She warned Rose that no one would marry a woman who stood out on the street making speeches: "Nice girls" didn't do that. And how would she ever find a husband when the labor movement took up all her time? In fact, Rose met many interesting men and fell in love easily, though none of the relationships ever led to marriage.

Rose Schneiderman knew that she was not leading a "normal" life for a woman, but she was driven by a feeling that she had an important mission to accomplish. Every day at factory closing time

Rose Schneiderman (fifth from the left) at a meeting of the Women's Trade Union League in 1910 during the shirt-waist-makers strike. Rose Schneiderman co-founded the first union of female workers in the garment industry and was the first woman elected to a leadership position in the trade union movement.

she left her job and went out onto the street to recruit union members. During lunch breaks she listened to workers' complaints or presented their grievances to the management. In the evenings she attended union meetings and political lectures.

Rose Schneiderman was no more than four and a half feet tall, but she had a powerful personality. She had the nerve to climb up on a ladder and speak out, the charisma to capture the attention of everyone around her, and the passion to draw them into her vision of justice for working people. She was such a powerhouse that one supporter of the WTUL offered her twenty-five dollars a week to work for the labor movement full-time. It was an amazing offer, but it meant not finishing high school, perhaps never becoming a teacher. Schneiderman hesitated, but she knew that her heart was in the trade union movement, and she decided to accept the position.

Rose Schneiderman's career as a professional labor organizer began in 1908, during a period of economic chaos on the Lower East Side. With their salaries at rock-bottom levels and their job security constantly threatened by layoffs, the workers often expressed their frustration by going out on strike. Strikes, also known as walkouts, can be powerful weapons for workers, but most unions were not yet strong enough to carry them off. Lacking adequate planning and leadership, the strikes would fizzle out, leaving the workers discouraged and embittered.

One of Schneiderman's goals was to show workers, especially women, how to use their collective weaponry more effectively. Going from shop to shop, she taught workers how to conduct their meetings, how to make group decisions, and how to present their complaints. When they went out on strike, she helped them to organize picket lines, state their demands, and negotiate with their employers.

During 1908 and 1909, Rose Schneiderman worked with many different groups in the garment trade: paper-box makers, white goods (underwear) workers, cap makers, and more. But her biggest challenge was to organize the thousands of women who were working in the shirtwaist industry.

The shirtwaist blouse was the hottest new item on the clothing market. Generally worn with a simple dark skirt, it was replacing the one-piece dress as the standard item of ladies' apparel. The shirtwaist had a high-buttoned collar, pleats across the front, and a fitted waistline. Practical, inexpensive, and comfortable, it represented the new personal freedom of women who were no longer confined to the home. Sadly, it was also to become a symbol of their exploitation.

The Uprising of the Twenty Thousand

By the year 1909, there were more than six hundred shirtwaist "shops" (as the factory workrooms were called) on the Lower East Side, with a labor force of some thirty-two thousand. About 70 percent of these workers were Jewish women. As the newest segment of the garment industry, the shirtwaist companies had better facilities than most of the other garment manufacturers. But their exploitation of workers, especially their female workers, was notorious.

Women in the shirtwaist industry put in as many as fourteen hours a day, usually on a piece-work basis. According to this system, the supervisors, who were always men, turned a profit based on the amount their "girls" produced. The women were paid less than any men who did the same work. They were also subject to the crude flirtations of their bosses. At the Triangle Shirtwaist Company, king of the shirtwaist makers, there were the added insults of being timed when they stopped work to use the toilet and having their handbags searched daily for stolen goods.

From factory to factory, Rose Schneiderman carried her message that shirtwaist workers could stand together against these injustices if they joined the trade union movement. But the threats of their powerful employers seemed to be holding them back. A breakthrough finally came in the summer of 1909, when the employees of the giant Triangle Shirtwaist Company voted to unionize. They also decided to affiliate with the United Hebrew Trades, another organization that was helping to establish trade unions in the garment industry.

Triangle's owners were set against a union in their shop, and they began to fire employees who were suspected of being union activists. But the tactic didn't work. The remaining employees not only went ahead and formed their union, they also stunned the industry by calling for an immediate strike against Triangle.

Nearly a thousand workers—all of them women—walked the

picket line. Week after week they crowded the sidewalk in front of Triangle's headquarters. The strikers looked to Rose Schneiderman for guidance, and she devoted herself to supporting them. But nothing she did could stop the threats and assaults by company-hired thugs. The police, as usual, seemed to side with the employers. They offered the strikers no protection and arrested them on phony charges, such as violating property and disturbing the peace.

In mid-November the Triangle strike was on the verge of collapse, and the ILGWU called an emergency meeting of shirtwaist workers. On November 22, some three thousand women crowded into the auditorium at Cooper Union for that historic event. A year before, these women were isolated individuals. Now, thanks to Rose Schneiderman's persistence, they were united in their common purpose.

The audience listened hopefully as labor and civic leaders called for unity, financial contributions, and moral support for the shirtwaist makers. Yet all the words seemed to be leading nowhere until a young woman in the audience stood up and asked to be heard.

The woman was Clara Lemlich, a Jewish immigrant who had

Shirtwaist makers on strike selling copies of The Call, *a socialist newspaper. Newspapers like the English* Call *and the Yiddish* Forward *were instrumental in bringing information to the immigrant population of the Lower East Side.*

gone to work in a factory at the age of fifteen, as soon as she arrived in the United States from Europe. Clara Lemlich, who worked for the Leiserson Company, had been a faithful participant in the Triangle strike. She had already been arrested seventeen times and had suffered six broken ribs from police beatings. Still she was not ready to give in. That night at Cooper Union the crowd became silent as she declared in her native Yiddish:

> I am a working girl, one of those striking against intolerable conditions. I am tired of listening to speakers who talk in generalities. What we are here for is to decide what to do about the strike. I offer a resolution that a general strike be declared—now.

Clara Lemlich was the catalyst, stirring her sister workers to take charge of their lives. But it was Rose Schneiderman who had brought them to the point where they were ready to do so, and it was she who took the responsibility for sustaining the strikers through a long and severe winter on the picket line.

Rose Schneiderman marched with the shirtwaist makers, and she assembled supporters of the Women's Trade Union League to join the picket line as well. Behind the scenes, she worked with a pool of volunteer lawyers who were ready to appear before the police or judges to keep the strikers out of jail. With 723 arrests in the first month alone, there was always a need for more funds to cover bail and court fees. To add to the money contributed locally, Schneiderman made a whirlwind fund-raising trip to Massachusetts. Rousing authorities at Faneuil Hall in Boston and at three prominent women's colleges—Radcliffe, Wellesley, and Mount Holyoke—she returned to New York with an additional ten thousand dollars for the strikers' fund.

Members of the audience burst into applause, leaping to their feet to demonstrate support for Lemlich's proposal that all shirtwaist makers in the city join the Triangle strike. When the meeting finally came to order, the chairman solemnly called on every woman present to raise her right hand and recite in unison the ancient Jewish vow of loyalty: "If I turn traitor to the cause I now pledge, may this hand wither from the arm I now raise."

The next morning more than twenty thousand shirtwaist makers from more than 150 shops joined forces in a citywide walkout. It was the first major workers' uprising that New York City had ever seen. And it was the first uprising of women in U.S. history.

Never had a strike aroused so much sympathy. Clergy delivered sermons in support of the workers. Social reformers and civic leaders spoke on their behalf. And newspaper coverage was generally favorable, drawing attention to a problem that many had known nothing about. All kinds of people were touched by the suffering and determination of these noble young women.

As the winter wore on, the shirtwaist manufacturers had to face reality: If the strike continued much longer, they would lose their entire spring production season. By mid-February 1910, the majority of factory owners were at last ready to settle with the workers and get on with their business. All but thirteen manufacturers agreed to some improvements in working conditions, a ten-hour cap on the workday, and at least a small raise in wages. Most important in the long run, however, was their acceptance of the general principle of collective bargaining—the idea that employers and workers should sit down together to work out their differences.

Throughout the Lower East Side there was a feeling of exhilaration in the air. Momentous changes were taking place as a result of the long strike. Membership in the Shirtwaist Makers Union had grown from a few hundred in November 1909 to ten thousand in February 1910, and it was still growing. The Uprising of the Twenty Thousand, as the shirtwaist makers' strike came to be known, infused the Jewish community with pride and excitement. The Uprising of the Twenty Thousand also inspired a series of other strikes in 1910, culminating in the Great Revolt of the Cloak Makers. This time it was the men who went out on strike, nearly sixty thousand of them. The women had shown them the way.

The Triangle Tragedy

One of the thirteen firms that did not settle with the shirtwaist makers was the Triangle Shirtwaist Company. In fact, after the strike, conditions at Triangle became harsher than ever. As if making up for the time and money lost during the strike, there were frequent speed-ups in production and an overall decline in wages. There were always fines to pay—fines for the slightest damage to a garment, for even a minute's lateness, for too many minutes spent in the toilet. And there were the blatant hazards to safety and health: factory doors kept locked during working hours, oily scraps of fabric heaped everywhere, workers crowded together.

As soon as the shirtwaist makers returned to their sewing machines, Rose Schneiderman renewed her efforts to build the union at Triangle. For the next year, that was her top priority, but it remained her most elusive goal. Then, suddenly, it was too late.

On Saturday afternoon, March 25, 1911, some eight hundred women and several dozen men were at work in Triangle's headquarters on the eighth, ninth, and tenth floors of the Asch Building near Washington Square. A few minutes before closing time at the end of another long work week, the careless toss of a cigarette ignited a pile of oily rags. The fire spread rapidly from one pile of scraps to another, and within minutes all three floors were in flames.

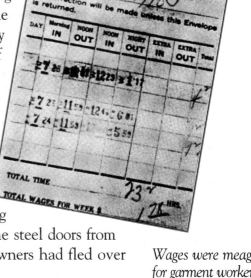

Firefighters rushed to the scene, but their tallest ladder—the tallest fire ladder in the city—did not reach above the seventh floor of the building. Their safety nets could not bear the impact of the many workers who jumped from so high to escape the consuming flames. Only one narrow exit was open, and the steel doors from the factory to the street remained locked. The owners had fled over the roof without bothering to open them.

It took less than half an hour to bring the fire under control, but the toll was staggering: 147 women and 21 men dead. Another 200 suffered broken limbs or critical burns. Cries of terror and grief filled the streets of the Lower East Side as people rushed toward the scene of the fire to see whether a loved one was among the bodies that lay on the sidewalk. Everyone, it seemed, knew someone who might have been there.

The day after the fire, the Shirtwaist Makers Union joined the WTUL, the Workmen's Circle (a Jewish fraternal organization), the

Wages were meager for garment workers, as shown by this pay envelope from the early 1900s.

Jewish Daily Forward (a Yiddish newspaper), and the American Red Cross to provide relief for the families of the victims, who were mostly Jewish and Italian immigrants between the ages of sixteen and twenty-three. All over the city people poured out their sympathy through donations to the relief fund, contributing more than $120,000 in all.

For the leaders of the unions involved, financial relief for the victims and their families was only a temporary solution to a chronic problem. To eliminate the problem, the union leaders would have to expose the outrageous conditions that had caused the Triangle disaster and press for legal assurances that such a catastrophe would never take place again. What was needed, they believed, was a massive protest rally to get the public on their side. Through the connections of a wealthy friend of the WTUL, the unions obtained permission to use the Metropolitan Opera House, where the city's most prestigious social and cultural events took place.

A Cry for Justice

A week later, on the evening of April 2, the great hall of the Met was filled with an unusual mix of people. East Side workers, most of them female, arrived early and packed the galleries. Seated in the orchestra and mezzanine were society ladies, suffragettes, social reformers, and other well-to-do people who had come to express their solidarity with the workers.

On the stage were clergy and civic leaders, who had come to urge that relief efforts for the families of the Triangle victims be continued. They spoke of the guilt shared by all members of society. They called for closer monitoring of fire regulations, more fire inspectors, and some sort of workers' compensation for work-related injuries. It was an agenda that might have pleased everyone present. But when the chair of the meeting presented a resolution on these points, there were shouts and hisses from the galleries and interruptions from the floor.

People were tired of resolutions being passed and never acted on. They said there would be no improvement if workers continued to rely on the good intentions of others. They insisted that workers be organized by districts so that they could form their own commit-

Opposite: Overcrowded workrooms filled with piles of flammable oily rags caused the tragic Triangle Fire that killed 168 garment workers (147 women and 21 men) on March 25, 1911.
Top: Lines of grieving relatives and friends identify the bodies of their loved ones.

tees and become a powerful voting bloc. They proposed that fire inspections be conducted by union officials themselves.

The shouting continued, the tension grew, and the meeting began to dissolve in chaos. But it was saved by a small red-haired woman in a drab brown dress who came from the background, slowly approaching the podium from her seat on the stage. Rose Schneiderman spoke with difficulty, trying hard to control her emotions. Yet the force of her spontaneous, heartfelt words held everyone spellbound. The next morning *The New York Times* recorded them for history:

> I would be a traitor to these poor burned bodies if I came here to talk good fellowship. We have tried you good people of the public and we have found you wanting. . . .
>
> This is not the first time girls have been burned alive in the city. Every week I must learn of the untimely death of one of my sister workers. Every year thousands of us are maimed. The life of men and women is so cheap and property is so sacred. There are so many of us for one job, it matters little if 143 of us are burned to death.
>
> We have tried you citizens; we are trying you now, and you have a couple of dollars for the sorrowing mothers and brothers and sisters by way of a charity gift. But every time the workers come out in the only way they know to protest against conditions which are unbearable, the strong hand of the law is allowed to press down heavily upon us.
>
> Public officials have only words of warning to us—warning that we must be intensely orderly and must be intensely peaceable. . . . The strong hand of the law beats us back when we rise [against] the conditions that make life unbearable.
>
> I can't talk fellowship to you who are gathered here. Too much blood has been spilled. I know from my experience, it is up to the working people to save themselves. The only way they can save themselves is by a strong working-class movement.

Rose Schneiderman spoke in a voice that was hardly above a whisper, but the silence was such that her words were heard in every corner of the vast opera hall.

The Cry Echoes

Rose Schneiderman shaking hands at a women's suffrage rally. Whether campaigning for safer and more humane working conditions or for women's suffrage, Rose Schneiderman fought for the rights of working women throughout her life.

Three days later, on April 5, Rose Schneiderman again touched the crowd as she marched through the streets of New York in the day-long funeral procession for the unidentified victims of the Triangle fire. More than a week after the fire, seven bodies remained unclaimed and unidentified, and union representatives had obtained permission from the city to hold a public funeral for them.

For three days Schneiderman had worked ceaselessly to make sure that notices of the funeral—in English, Yiddish, and Italian—got into the hands of workers throughout the Lower East Side and Brooklyn. Now the outpouring of solidarity was overwhelming. According to police estimates, about 126,000 people, mostly women, marched behind the horse-drawn hearses; another 275,000 people lined the sidewalks as the procession passed.

It was a miserable, rainy day, but among the silent marchers there was hardly a raincoat or an umbrella to be seen. Rose Schneiderman walked solemnly near the front of the procession, without even a hat for protection. At one point she stumbled and fell behind, appearing near collapse. Two colleagues, Mary Dreier, president of the WTUL, and Helen Marot, the organization's secretary, came swiftly to the rescue. Lifting her from either side, they held on to her arms, and the three women continued along the way.

As the procession moved down Fifth Avenue, the crowds recognized the "girl" who was being helped along by her friends. She was the one who had given that speech at the Met, the one who had been giving speeches everywhere since the terrible day of the fire. Her name passed through the crowd as people pressed closer to the curb to catch a glimpse of the courageous little woman who spoke so powerfully for all the poor factory girls of New York.

In the aftermath of the Triangle fire, Rose Schneiderman's cry for justice echoed all over New York City. It was heard all the way up in the state capital, Albany, where the governor appointed the State Factory Investigating Commission. As an officer of the WTUL, Schneiderman appeared as a witness before the commission and offered many recommendations for the greater protection of women workers.

The first report of the State Factory Investigating Commission, issued in 1912, recommended a new Industrial Code, a set of standards and regulations to protect the health and safety of all workers in factories and commercial businesses. In 1913, that code was enacted into law by the New York state legislature.

Over the decades Rose Schneiderman continued to play a major role in every battle for the rights of working women: minimum wages, equal pay for equal work, unemployment insurance, pregnancy compensation, and of course safety in the workplace. But she always regarded the New York Industrial Code with special pride, for it was, in her own words, "a living monument to those 143 women whose lives were sacrificed in the Triangle Fire."

In her long tenure as president of the Women's Trade Union League (1926–1950) and its New York chapter (1918–1949), Rose Schneiderman remained a national spokesperson for and advocate of workers' rights. When she died, in 1972, The New York Times remembered her as the person who "did more to upgrade the dignity and living standards of working women than any other American."

CHAPTER 2

Henrietta Szold
MOTHER OF MULTITUDES
(1860–1945)

*B*orn in Baltimore in 1860, Henrietta Szold was raised in a cultured, middle-class Jewish home. Sophie and Rabbi Benjamin Szold, who came to America from Hungary, were able to provide their children with the comforts and educational advantages that most eastern European immigrants never had. As the oldest child in a family of daughters, Henrietta had the privilege of studying with her father. Her knowledge of Jewish *subjects was so great that she was admitted to the Jewish Theological Seminary in New York City as a "special student," becoming the first woman to study rabbinic texts at the all-male institution. She also served as the first editor of the Jewish Publication Society, earning the respect of many scholars and writers.*

Henrietta Szold was already in her fifties when the focus of her life changed from scholarship to Zionism, the rebirth of Jewish life in Palestine. With her rare blend of idealism, drive, and compassion, she succeeded in bringing modern medical care to Palestine, developing a wide range of educational programs, and setting up a system of social services for the struggling inhabitants of a far-from-modern land. But the project that filled the last decade of her life was, to her, the most rewarding of all.

*W*hen Henrietta Szold returned from her first trip to Palestine in 1909, she couldn't stop thinking about the children: children wandering about in rags, children begging in the streets, children suffering from diseases like trachoma, whose victims' infected eyes attracted ugly black flies. She was haunted by these images of poverty, and in her heart was a burning determination to do something about it.

As with most of the problems that Henrietta Szold would encounter over the next three decades in Palestine, it never occurred to her that it might not be possible to find a solution. She began with her own Hadassah Study Circle, a small group of Zionist women in New York City. Sparing no details, she described the deprivation she had seen in the slums of Palestine—the poor, pious Jews suffering from lack of sanitation, hygiene, and basic medical care. It was time, she urged, to turn their Zionism into action and come to the aid of these struggling people.

Before long Szold's study circle joined with others to form a national organization called Hadassah, the first official organization of Zionist women. At their first convention, held in 1912, the women elected Henrietta Szold as their president. They chose as their motto, "the healing of the daughter of my people," and, with Henrietta Szold leading the way, began to raise money to bring better health care to the people of Palestine.

Henrietta Szold's involvement with Zionism was not new. She had been a hardworking Zionist since 1893—even before the First Zionist Congress, in 1897, called for the resettlement of the Jewish homeland. She was the only woman in the inner circle of Zionist leadership in America and secretary of the Federation of American Zionists.

Her work for the Zionist movement was so highly valued that a group of friends raised the funds to provide her with an annual income for the rest of her life. With this financial security, she resigned from her job as editor at the Jewish Publication Society and devoted herself to her new calling.

Over the next few years Henrietta Szold worked incessantly to set up chapters of Hadassah and raise enough money to send the first American Zionist Medical Unit to Palestine. The group of twenty doctors and nurses, which she personally selected and organized, set sail in 1918. Two years later, at age fifty-nine, she joined them in Palestine and became the director of the medical unit. The following year she opened the doors of a nursing school, where local residents—Jews and Arabs alike—could be trained to serve the local population.

Henrietta Szold believed passionately in the right of Jews to resettle Palestine, but she cared less about a Jewish state than about the health and safety of all the people who lived there. To her the most important thing was for Jews and Arabs to learn to live with one another. Otherwise, she believed, no one would survive.

Henrietta Szold poses with the first graduating class of Hadassah nurses in 1922.

The Stubborn Old Girl

Most of the Zionist leaders in Palestine did not share Szold's political ideas. Sometimes they called her "the old girl" and complained about her stubbornness. But they also admired her accomplishments and so elected her to the highest positions of Zionist leadership. Often, it seemed, they gave her the hardest jobs.

In 1927, Henrietta Szold was named to the three-person executive committee of the World Zionist Organization and given overall responsibility for health and education in Palestine. In 1931, she was one of seven people elected by the the general assembly of Palestinian Jewry (Vaad Leumi) to oversee the beginnings of Jewish self-government. Now her job was to transfer the administration of health, welfare, and education programs from the Zionist organizations abroad to local authorities in Palestine. It was a huge and complicated assignment, but she undertook it with enthusiasm—because it had to be done! Within a short time the population of Palestine had a system of local services, which remained intact until 1948 and is the heart of the social service system in Israel today.

Still at the root of her work in Palestine was Szold's concern for the impoverished children, particularly those whom other officials called "juvenile delinquents." The ruling British authorities wanted to punish these youths as they would ordinary criminals, but Szold understood that their problems resulted from poverty, idleness, and lack of education.

Henrietta Szold poured her heart into programs for these children—hygiene instruction, health screenings, vocational training, and more. But she neared the end of her term knowing there was still much more to be done. And she was running out of energy. Now in her seventies, she felt it was time to wind down her activities in Palestine. She thought about doing some work with Hadassah in America. After living alone in Jerusalem for more than a decade, she was longing to be with her family again.

Then in the summer of 1933, Szold received a proposal that set an unexpected course for the rest of her life. The proposal came from Recha Freier, the wife of a rabbi in Berlin. Troubled by the decline of Jewish life in Germany, Freier wanted to send groups of German Jewish youths to agricultural settlements (kibbutzim) in

Palestine, where they would have the chance to live meaningful Jewish lives. Would Henrietta Szold, as head of education and welfare services in Palestine, give the plan her blessing? Would she come to Berlin and help organize the program?

No, she would not. Szold was perplexed by the idea of setting up a program especially for young German Jews when the needs of the slum children were so great. Wasn't her first responsibility to the thousands of deprived children already in Palestine? Ten thousand of them still received no education. Why not take some of those children to kibbutzim and give them a new way of life?

The young German Jews, by comparison, had all the advantages of education, good homes, and a decent standard of living. Why take them away from their families and plunge them into the chaos and hardships of Palestine? Why expose them to the random outbreaks of violence against the Jews? She was sure these people in Berlin did not understand what life in Palestine was like. But neither did anyone in Palestine understand what danger was looming for the Jews of Germany.

The "stubborn old girl" at work. Henrietta Szold's determination and strong will enabled her to save the lives of thousands of Jewish children.

Henrietta Szold politely dismissed the proposal from Germany. But when Recha Freier went ahead and located a kibbutz that was willing to take one of her groups, Szold reconsidered. If there was going to be such a program, she wanted it to go well, and she did not want it to be separate from the other youth programs she had created. Szold decided to delay her trip to the United States—just for a few months—and go to Germany instead.

The Only Person for the Job

Henrietta Szold arrived in Berlin in October 1933 and quickly saw why the German Jews needed her help. In the lobby of her hotel that first day, all activity came to a standstill for the broadcast of a speech by Adolf Hitler, who was campaigning to become chancellor of Germany. Szold stood trembling as people all around her responded with shouts of "Heil Hitler!" and curses on "Die Juden!" Now she understood why Jewish parents would send their children to Palestine. She unpacked and got to work.

Szold spent a week in Berlin, working with organizers of the Jüdische Jugendhilfe (Society to Aid Jewish Youth) to develop a plan for the youth immigration. "I don't flatter myself that I straightened out the whole tangle," she wrote afterward, "but I think the path is somewhat leveled." It was a typical understatement of her own accomplishments. What she produced that week was nothing less than a full-scale blueprint for Youth Aliyah. It was a plan that would be followed for decades.

The first step was to set up training farms in the rural outskirts of Berlin where young Jews would gather for six-week courses on Zionism and agricultural life. After six weeks, those who were ready for *aliyah*, living in Palestine, would be organized into groups of fifty and assigned a leader. Each group would travel to an agricultural settlement in Palestine and remain there together for two years while learning the language and the ways of their new country.

Henrietta Szold was pleased to return to Jerusalem with a plan so well crafted. But she was not happy to learn that in her absence the Jewish Agency had created an official department for Youth Aliyah and had designated her to serve as its head. She had not been consulted, and she had other matters to consider. Wasn't she entitled to a break, to some time with her family? She did not want to postpone her trip to the United States indefinitely.

Szold explained her concerns to Arthur Ruppin, the Jewish Agency official who brought her the news, but he simply ignored her protests. "With you or not at all," he stated flatly. She was the only person who could handle this assignment, he said, "the only non-political person of stature," the only one who could deal with all the political parties and with the British authorities as well.

Henrietta Szold was a proud woman who did not like to be manipulated, but Ruppin's argument had been effective. She put aside her good reasons for not accepting the position and followed her heart's desire, to be there for the children.

"I should have had children—many children," she had written many years earlier to one of her close friends in the United States. But the opportunity for marriage and a family of her own had passed her by. Now, at an age when most women are grandmothers and in retirement, Henrietta Szold was becoming the mother of multitudes. And Ruppin was right: She was the perfect person for the job.

The Old Lady and Her Children

There was no time to waste. The first Youth Aliyah group would arrive early in 1934, and it was already November of 1933. There were only a few months to go, and there was everything to do—raising funds, obtaining British immigration certificates, building the bunks where the children would sleep, and hiring the teachers, nurses, and social workers who would guide and care for them.

With the help of her much younger assistant, Emma Ehrlich, Szold supervised every detail. And she worried all the time. To her friend Rose Jacobs she wrote that the youth immigration was "an undertaking so overwhelmingly responsible" that she "sometimes wanted to run away." She wrote, too, that it might well be the most worthwhile thing she had ever done.

When the first Youth Aliyah group arrived in Haifa on February 19, 1934, Henrietta Szold was waiting on the wharf. It was an emotional moment, seeing the ship approach with forty-three young passengers—forty-three young lives now entrusted to her. As the children stepped off the gangplank, the white-haired woman

Henrietta Szold insisted on visiting the Youth Aliyah children on their settlements in Palestine, despite the primitive roads and the danger of attacks by Arab snipers.

greeted each one with a kindly smile and a twinkle in her eye. She wanted the children to know they could count on her.

From Haifa she traveled with the children to the town of Athlit, to see them through customs and their medical examinations. Then she accompanied them to their new home, En Harod, near the Sea of Galilee. For the next two days she tromped around the muddy kibbutz in her proper hat and dark dress, making sure everything was in order. She checked the mattresses, the mosquito netting, the toilets, and the showers. And she spent time with each child, leaving them all with the assurance of her personal interest.

Heartened by this first experience, Szold made the long bus trip back to Jerusalem to proceed with preparations for the next group. When the children of the Ahavah orphanage arrived in Palestine two months later, she was again waiting at the dock. And until the last year of her life, Szold welcomed each new group just as she welcomed the first. All over the country she was known affectionately as the charming old lady who meets the ships.

Szold also wrote regularly to the children, and she answered each of their letters personally. She worried about their individual problems and illnesses, and she spent two days a week visiting them in the settlements. Travel was not easy in those days, especially for a woman in her seventies. It was dangerous, too, with Arab snipers posted along the roads, waiting to ambush Jewish travelers. But Szold never hesitated. When it came to her children, she spared herself no energy and avoided no risk. During one hot and muggy week in August 1935, she managed to see all six hundred of her charges.

With these visits fresh in her mind, Henrietta Szold traveled to Switzerland to report to the annual meeting of the Zionist Congress on the first eighteen months of Youth Aliyah. Hoping to convince the delegates that this new movement deserved their continued support, she was taken by surprise when they greeted her with long and thunderous applause.

Judenraus!

Immediately after the Zionist Congress, Henrietta Szold went to Amsterdam for the first conference of Youth Aliyah International, where the delegates agreed that it was time to expand their activities into Poland and other countries. Then it was on to Berlin, this time with Emma Ehrlich as her companion, to confer again with her German partners.

Two years had passed since Henrietta Szold's first trip to Berlin, and she was horrified by the changes that had taken place. With Palestine so isolated and mail from Germany censored, it was difficult to know what was really going on. Now she saw for herself that the country was raging with anti-Semitism. Her arrival coincided with the announcement of the infamous Nuremburg Laws, which stripped the Jews of their German citizenship and turned them into social outcasts. Calls of "Judenraus!" (Out with the Jews!) were in the air.

Traveling into the countryside to visit some of the Youth Aliyah training farms, Szold saw signs by the road that declared JEWS NOT WELCOME HERE! and BEWARE OF JEWS—THEY WILL RUIN YOUR DAUGHTERS. Clearly, the training farms could not continue in this environment; they would have to be reestablished in another country—perhaps Holland, France, England, or Scandinavia.

Henrietta Szold stayed in Berlin for a month. During that time she met with Eva Stern, who was running the Jüdische Jugendhilfe office; with other staff members and group leaders; and with Jewish parents and children. She was inspired by the courage and dignity that all these Jews displayed. In the midst of so much tension, they carried on with the lunches, teas, and dinners that had been planned in her honor. Her hosts were endlessly grateful for the presence of this tiny old woman. To them, Henrietta Szold represented the concern of the outside world and the possibility of deliverance— at least for their children. But when she returned to Berlin again two years later, that hope seemed to have died. The Jews, she reported, were like living corpses, paralyzed by fear.

After her visits to Berlin, Szold had a new sense of urgency concerning Youth Aliyah. The situation of Jewish youth in Europe was changing dramatically. Her work was no longer a matter of giving them a more positive Jewish life; it was a matter of ensuring their survival.

With the cloud of war about to burst over Europe, the goal of Youth Aliyah was to get young Jews out of Germany and its neighboring countries as quickly as possible. While the Arabs in Palestine were pressuring the British to let fewer Jews in, Henrietta Szold kept making requests for more certificates of immigration. To her great relief, the British announced in March 1938 that there would be no restriction on youth immigration for the next six months.

A day later the Nazis marched into Austria, and practically overnight the situation of the Jews became even more perilous. Without even thinking about the danger to herself, Szold decided to go immediately to Vienna, the Austrian capital, to set up a Youth Aliyah operation. But her plans were halted abruptly by a warning from Adolf Eichmann, the same Eichmann who was later executed in Jerusalem for his inhumane crimes against the Jews. Eichmann declared that Henrietta Szold was "not to attempt to set foot in Austria." He also stormed into the Youth Aliyah office in Berlin and demanded that the emigration work cease.

By August 1939, approximately thirty-five hundred Jewish children had been brought to Palestine by Youth Aliyah, and another three hundred certificate holders were waiting in Germany. Within days these three hundred children were whisked out of

Germany. But by September 1, when Hitler invaded Poland, Europe was officially at war and the usual routes to Palestine were blocked. Most means of transportation were taken over by the military, ships

were scarce, and fares were outrageously high. Nevertheless, with the help of friends in Holland and Denmark, the Youth Aliyah children were moved through Europe and onto ships headed for Palestine. Over the next two years another seven hundred came out of Germany, but by the spring of 1941, Germany and all German-held territories were closed to emigration. Two million Jewish children remained in Nazi-occupied Europe.

Town to Village

Life in Palestine during the war years was lonely and harsh. The interruption of normal trade resulted in economic crisis. There were shortages of food and of the supplies needed for building and industry. Unemployment swept the country. The political situation

Anti-Semitism in Germany escalated during the 1930s. On the evening of November 9, 1938, Jewish synagogues, homes, and businesses were systematically set on fire and looted. This became known as Kristallnacht, "the Night of Broken Glass."

was also tense, with outbreaks of Arab violence against Jews and conflict among the various Zionist political parties. Information from Europe and America was scarce.

The U.S. government advised its citizens to leave Palestine, but Szold no longer thought of leaving. She wouldn't even consider it. She had to stay with her children. There were the thousands already in Youth Aliyah, and there were the children who she believed would eventually come out of Europe.

In the meantime there were also the street children of the Palestinian slums, the ones whose plight had drawn her to Palestine in the first place. With immigration down to a trickle and hundreds of Youth Aliyah facilities standing empty, why not make the program available to children from poor urban families? Szold once again brought the idea to Hadassah, which had adopted Youth Aliyah as one of its projects. This time the organization agreed to give it a chance.

The Town to Village experiment was launched that spring with Henrietta Szold's usual careful planning. She began on a small scale, with sixty youngsters divided into three groups. Each group would

∞

Youth Aliyah children depart from Berlin in 1935. These youth had spent six weeks preparing for their new life in Palestine.

be sent to a settlement of Youth Aliyah graduates, where Eastern and Western Jews could live and work together. That summer, when Jewish refugees from Syria and Yemen began to pour into Palestine, she quickly brought 750 of their children into the program as well. Eventually, the experiment became an ongoing program for thousands of participants, and today it is the main activity of Youth Aliyah.

Henrietta Szold could surely find satisfaction in seeing that opportunities were brighter for the children of Palestine, but for Jewish children in Europe, life was a darkening nightmare. If anyone in Palestine knew then that Jewish children were being systematically murdered by Hitler, Szold was not among them. Nor could she ever have acknowledged that human beings were capable of such cruelty.

The Children of War

The reality began to be known in the fall of 1942, when the Jewish Agency learned of the mass arrival of fourteen thousand refugees from Poland at a Red Cross camp outside Tehran, in Iran. Shortly after the fall of Warsaw to the German army, these refugees had begun to wander eastward, desparate to escape from Nazi-occupied territories. For three years they had traveled by foot, scavenging for food and shelter. Thousands died along the way, and the survivors were barely alive. A Jewish Agency official rushed to the camp and reported that among the throngs of refugees were hundreds of Jewish children.

The Jews of Palestine took the Tehran children into their hearts. Teachers, nurses, and social workers rushed to the Iranian camp while Szold went to work arranging for them to come to Palestine. She needed immigration certificates from the British, money from Hadassah, and, most difficult to obtain, a viable travel route. Neither Iraq nor Turkey would permit the Jewish children to travel across its land. Finally, Hadassah prevailed on the British Embassy in Washington, D.C., to arrange safe transport across the Persian

The children who arrived in Tehran from Poland in 1943 were withdrawn and fearful. They were children of war, who had seen starvation, destruction, and death.

Gulf, from Karachi, Pakistan, to Suez, in Egypt. Hans Beyth, Szold's closest associate, would meet the children in Suez and escort them by train the rest of the way to Palestine.

Finally, in February 1943, the Tehran children—933 in all—came home to Palestine. Szold's spirits rose when she saw their little blue-and-white flags waving from the windows of the approaching train, but the sight of the children who stepped onto the platform was heart-breaking. They did not look like any children she had ever seen. They were withdrawn, fearful, and wild looking—children of all ages dressed in odd pieces of scavenged clothing, children who did not smile. Now they were her children, and she would do everything she could for them.

For the Jews of Palestine, the story of the Tehran refugees was a hint of the horror that was taking place in Europe. By the end of 1942, the worst was confirmed: A cable from Zionist leaders in America reported that Hitler's destruction of the Jews was under way. Two million were already dead. Jewish appeals for intervention were brought to the Red Cross, to the pope, and to leaders of the free world, but no action resulted. President Franklin D. Roosevelt and British Prime Minister Winston Churchill said that the best way to stop the killing was to win the war quickly. No one, it seems, responded adequately. Even in Palestine, there was a reluctance to face the facts. In the newspapers of Jerusalem and Tel Aviv, reports of the mass killings of Jews were brief, vague, and skeptical. Another four million Jews died before it was over.

Henrietta Szold did not live to see the end of the war. She never knew that one and a half million Jewish children were murdered by the Nazis. She did know that Youth Aliyah had given new life to more than ten thousand Jewish children and that it was ready to embrace thousands more. They came as soon as the war ended, fifteen thousand between 1945 and 1948. After May 1948, when Palestine became the State of Israel, there was no limit to the number of Jewish children who could make it their home.

The Tehran children were the last group that Henrietta Szold welcomed personally. She returned to Jerusalem with a case of bronchitis that would not go away, and for the next two years she remained in poor health. When she could no longer travel around the country to visit the Youth Aliyah settlements, the children returned her many years of love with their letters and handmade gifts. Some of them, especially the graduates, managed to travel to Jerusalem to see her. A lovely young girl, one of the Tehran children, came each day to brush her long hair.

When Henrietta Szold died, on February 13, 1945, the nation mourned the loss of a great leader, a woman known and loved all over Palestine and throughout the Jewish world. Thousands followed her body in a procession to the ancient Jewish cemetery on the Mount of Olives, and one of the Tehran children led the recitation of the Mourners' Kaddish at her grave. It was the honor that would have pleased Szold most.

Hadassah continues to be one of the strongest Zionist organizations in the United States. True to the spirit of its founder, Henrietta Szold, the focus of Hadassah's work in Israel remains child welfare and medical care. Hadassah's two hospitals in Jerusalem, along with its medical, dental, and nursing schools, continue to provide the highest-quality treatment for Jews and Arabs of the region. The programs of Youth Aliyah provide fresh opportunities for thousands of Jewish children each year.

CHAPTER 3

Zivia Lubetkin
GHETTO COMMANDER
(1914–1978)

*I*n the spring of 1946, a weary and somber young woman named Zivia Lubetkin arrived in Palestine, where she was already something of a legend. Zivia had an amazing story to tell, and settlers from all over Palestine gathered at a special meeting to hear her tell it. It was a story of the unimaginable: a small group of Zionist youth in the Warsaw ghetto rising up against the mighty German army. Zivia spoke for hours, providing *a complete firsthand account of that heroic uprising but never drawing attention to the central role she herself played in it.*

Born into the narrow world of the eastern European shtetl, Zivia Lubetkin emerged as a wartime leader of the Zionist youth movement, a founder of the Jewish Fighting Organization, and a commander of the armed revolt. But to Jews all over Poland she was simply "Zivia," the brave and compassionate woman whom they called the Mother of the Ghetto.

On the evening of December 31, 1939, a group of friends from the Zionist youth movement in Poland came together in Lvov, a city in the Ukraine, to bring in the new year. On the surface it might have seemed like any other New Year's Eve party or youth conference, but these young people were only pretending to celebrate. Four months earlier the German army had marched into Poland, Europe was now at war, and crucial questions about the future of their movement had to be faced.

Could the Zionist youth movement survive the anti-Semitic restrictions and persecutions of the Nazi regime? What could these young people—none of them over thirty—possibly accomplish? There was no way for them to know for sure, but they were determined to carry on. As members of the central committee of He-Halutz ("the pioneer"), they resolved to rebuild their movement "underground," quietly conducting activities in the areas under German occupation. Theirs was a renewed pledge to keep the Zionist flame burning.

Among this small group of idealists was Zivia Lubetkin. Born in the small town of Bitan in eastern Poland, Zivia was determined to leave the shtetl behind and fulfill the Zionist dream of settling in Palestine. As a teenager she joined the He-Halutz branch of the Zionist youth movement and soon became a valued leader. She organized educational programs and training farms to prepare other young Jews for a new way of life in their own land.

When the Germans entered Poland on September 1, 1939, Zivia was staying at 34 Dzielna Street in Warsaw, a center of activity for

He-Halutz. A week later she was called to Soviet-occupied eastern Poland to help establish escape routes to Palestine while it was still possible to do so. Traveling from town to town, she directed Jews to head south to the Romanian border or north to Vilna. But she herself chose to remain in Poland, where there was so much work to be done.

Zivia went wherever the movement needed her, and as 1939 ticked away, it became clear what her next destination would be. An urgent message had arrived from Frumka Plotnitzka, who was managing He-Halutz affairs in Warsaw with the help of another young woman, Leah Perilstein. They needed Zivia there. The central committee considered the request and everyone was in agreement: Zivia must return to Warsaw.

The next evening, Zivia was at the train station, saying a tearful good-bye to her friends, all of them about to leave for other cities and towns where Jewish lives were in danger. As the train to Bialystok pulled away from the station, Zivia tried to imagine Warsaw after four months of German occupation. There were such terrible stories about the Nazis' treatment of the Jews—she didn't know whether she could bear it.

The first leg of the trip went smoothly enough. A messenger was waiting in Bialystok, and he arranged for Zivia to cross the border with a group of Polish students who had been caught in the Soviet zone when war broke out. Setting out together under the cover of darkness, they trekked through the night, sometimes knee-deep in snow. Finally, at the border village of Malkinia, they crossed unnoticed into the German zone. Exhausted and relieved, the hikers collapsed at the train station to await the departure of the train to Warsaw.

After a few minutes of rest, Zivia noticed a group of Jews huddled together in a corner of the station as if they were hiding. At that moment a German man spotted them also, and he began shouting that Jews should not be allowed in the same waiting room with Poles and Germans. Zivia's companions joined the rumble, and the whole gang of them succeeded in chasing the Jews from the station.

Zivia was badly shaken. Now that they were in German-held territory, the Polish students were behaving very differently. She boarded the train with them, still frightened by the scene she had just witnessed. Throughout the night she heard loud, ugly voices shouting insults at Jewish passengers. At one point there were

Opposite: After the German army invaded Poland, Jews were taken from their villages and forced to live in enclosed areas of cities, called ghettos.

screams, and she realized that a Jew had been thrown from the moving train.

As the train lurched into Warsaw the next morning, Zivia stared out at the crowds on the streets. At first she was surprised by how normal the people looked. Then she noticed the Jews among them. They were easy to spot, each wearing the required badge of shame: a blue star of David on a white armband. They moved quickly, nervously, looking down or glancing over their shoulders like people who had no right to be there.

Overwhelmed by the task ahead of her, Zivia somehow found the strength to hold on to her own sense of dignity. Resolving to hold her head high, she made her way through the streets of Warsaw to the Jewish neighborhood and climbed the stairs of 34 Dzielna Street.

The Liaison Women

Before the war the house on Dzielna Street had been a movement "kibbutz," a place where dozens of He-Halutz leaders lived cooperatively, sharing the tasks of daily life as they would on a kibbutz in Palestine. Now there were hundreds of Jews under that same roof— Jews from all over Poland who had drifted to the capital city because they were unable to cross into the Soviet zone. Many of them had come from similar kibbutzim that had collapsed after the German invasion.

At the center of these people was Frumka Plotnitzka. She made room for whoever came, organizing and reorganizing to accommodate the displaced young Jews. She worried about meals, jobs, and cultural programs, responding to each new challenge with amazing energy. Like Zivia Lubetkin, Frumka Plotnitzka never looked for prestige or power. Yet the more she gave of herself, the greater was the esteem in which she was held.

With their light hair and fair complexion, Frumka Plotnitzka and Leah Perilstein were part of a special group of couriers, or messengers, known as the "liaison (or go-between) women." Since Jews could not move about easily outside the ghetto, the movement's travel missions had to be carried out by people who could pass for Poles. That meant looking like a gentile and speaking Polish like a Pole. Being a woman was also an advantage, for women traveling alone seemed to arouse less suspicion than did men.

The liaison women took great risks in order to carry out their assignments. They carried news and messages from ghetto to ghetto; smuggled food, weapons, and money; and brought warnings of approaching danger. They also searched for new farm sites in the countryside and set up bases for partisan fighters, Jews and Poles who were hiding out in the forests preparing for armed revolt against the Nazis. Without these women there would have been no coordinated effort; there would have been no communication at all.

With her dark coloring and classic Jewish features, Zivia was not a good candidate for travel missions. But her pure devotion to Zionism combined with her strong practical skills and steady character made her the perfect person to organize the comings and goings at Dzielna Street headquarters. Soon she turned the house into a thriving center for a wide network of underground activities in the German zone. These activities fell into three categories: the continued search for escape routes to Palestine, the revival of the training farms, and the creation of cultural and educational programs for Jews of all ages. The single overriding goal was to save the Jewish youth.

L. Kozabrodska, B. Chazan, and T. Schneiderman. Three Jewish "liaison women" who smuggled food, weapons, and money into the ghettos, and brought warnings of approaching danger.

At the same time, Zivia believed that the movement's primary day-to-day responsibility had to be humanitarian aid—a piece of bread and a hot meal for any hungry Jew who roamed the ghetto streets. As the war progressed, more and more Jews expelled from their towns and villages throughout Poland arrived homeless and jobless in Warsaw. So Zivia opened the doors to the soup kitchen even wider and organized the youth to feed as many as three hundred to four hundred people each day.

The organization of so many activities was remarkable in itself, but finding the financial means to support them was an even greater challenge. A little money came from the kibbutz movement in Palestine, but providing for all the people who came to depend on Zivia was a daily struggle. In order to gather funds, Zivia got to know everyone in the ghetto. She visited the Jewish organizations regularly, attended all kinds of meetings, waited in corridors, knocked on doors. She did whatever had to be done to get the food or money she needed.

With so much to do to provide emergency assistance, Zivia quickly realized she needed another person at Dzielna Street, some-one to concentrate on education and culture. She sent her request to the He-Halutz central committee, and the person selected was Yitzhak Zuckerman, one of the movement's most respected leaders. Zivia had met Yitzhak Zuckerman at the 1935 Zionist Congress in Switzerland and again at the New Year's Eve conference in Lvov. Eventually they married, but they never allowed their personal relationship to take priority over their assignments. To do so would have violated a fundamental principle of their movement: that the welfare of the community takes precedence over the personal desires of individuals.

The Terrible Truth

When Yitzhak Zuckerman arrived in Warsaw, he was impressed by all that Zivia had accomplished. But the overall condition of the Jews was deteriorating. In November 1940, the Germans completed the construction of ghetto walls, enclosing a neighbor-hood in which some 50,000 Jews had lived before the war. Now 300,000 Jews were squeezed inside that same area. As the roundups of Jews continued, the ghetto population swelled to nearly 500,000. Residents suffered terribly from overcrowding, disease, and hunger. Hundreds, sometimes thousands, died in a single day. Others were sent off to labor camps, from which they never returned.

And still the worst was not known. Throughout history Jews had experienced pogroms, persecutions, and expulsions. But there had never been a plan for the total annihilation of the Jewish people. It was unimaginable, even to those who were in the thick of the Nazi terror. By the end of 1941, however, reports of the unimaginable had begun to reach the ghetto.

They heard it first from Tema Schneiderman, one of the brave liaison women, who believed that the rumors of mass murder could no longer be ignored. Then Chaika Grossman came from Vilna to tell Zivia that she had seen it with her own eyes: an outright massacre of Jews in the area of Ponary, just outside Vilna. In January a Jew who had escaped from Chelmno reported that the Jews were being taken out of town by the truckload and murdered by poisonous gas. Shortly before Passover, Lonka Kozibrodska returned from one of her missions with news of the deportation of the Jews of Lublin and their execution at Belzec. The overall pattern could not be denied: It was a deliberate, organized attempt to wipe out the Jews. It was the wholesale, planned murder of an entire people, their own people.

For Yitzhak Zuckerman, who learned that members of his own family were among the Jews deported from Lublin, the reports were so shocking that he was barely able to function. What was the point of his activities, he asked, if they were all doomed to this terrible death? But Zivia would not let him give up. She, too, felt despair, yet she never stopped working. Once again she searched for the inner strength to keep going. And what kept her going, she later explained, was the feeling that there was still a special purpose to their life, their work, and even their death. "We had a reason to stand up and fight," she wrote. "There were people we had to defend. We could not commit suicide. The inner logic of youthful idealism compelled us to continue our efforts."

Gradually, Yitzhak recovered from the shock, and in the spring of 1942 he called on all the Zionist youth groups in the ghetto to form a resistance organization. Most of the Jews in Warsaw did not take to the idea that they should stand up and fight the Nazis. It was hard for them to admit that all the Jews would otherwise be murdered. Most still believed it possible to hold out quietly and survive the war. Many feared that the Germans would be even more brutal if the Jews organized to defend themselves. And some believed that their fate was in God's hands alone.

Nonetheless, the leaders of He-Halutz and Ha-Shomer Ha-Tza'ir, the two largest youth groups in the ghetto, decided to begin training their members. To do so, they needed weapons, and Zivia set to work finding the people who could supply them and the money to pay for them. She sent word to the Polish government-in-exile in London, but its leaders did not want to waste their resources on Jews. They said the Jews wouldn't defend themselves, that they would go to their deaths like sheep being led to slaughter. The Armia Krajowa, the major force in the Polish underground, was also suspicious of the Jews' request and would provide no help. Finally, the Armia Ludowa, a smaller Polish resistance group under the Communist Party, offered the Jews eight hand grenades. But the grenades never got to the ghetto; Lonka Kozibrodska was arrested while smuggling them in under her skirt.

A serious and idealistic couple, Zivia Lubetkin and her husband, Yitzhak Zuckerman were leading strategists of the uprising in the Warsaw ghetto.

Consequently, when the Germans surrounded the ghetto on July 22, 1942, the Jewish fighters had only two guns. It was the beginning of the *Aktion*—the mass deportation of the Jews of Warsaw—and there was no possibility of armed Jewish resistance.

The Germans ordered the Jewish ghetto police, their lackeys, to round up all the Jews and bring them to the large open area just inside the ghetto entrance. There the selections were made: who would live and who would die. Those who had jobs, either in factories within the ghetto or with work forces that were taken outside the ghetto each day, were allowed to remain. The others were to be "resettled" in an area where, they were told, there were plenty of jobs waiting for them. By the end of the first day, Zivia and Yitzhak had learned the true destination of the transports: the notorious death camp at Treblinka.

Once again, Yitzhak Zuckerman called together the representatives of the youth groups and pleaded for the formation of a Jewish resistance force. This time they were ready. On July 28, 1942, the Jewish Fighting Organization (JFO) was officially established, dedicated to the principle of Jewish self-defense. The founders vowed they would not go to their deaths without fighting back.

Meanwhile the *Aktion* continued, with thousands of Jews deported each day. By the middle of September, only about 75,000 Jews remained in the ghetto. Some 300,000 had been sent to Treblinka or were murdered on the spot.

Zivia Lubetkin and Yitzhak Zuckerman called a meeting of the organization to assess the situation. The survivors of the *Aktion* were in a state of mourning, believing that their deaths, too, were inevitable. What, then, could they do? Someone proposed that they go to their deaths in a final dramatic act: that they use their supply of gasoline to set huge fires and then attack the Germans with whatever they had— sticks, stones, their bare hands. It would be an act of collective suicide but perhaps a more dignified death than what the Germans had in store for them.

All through the night they debated the proposal: By morning they had dismissed it as a meaningless gesture. They could not turn away from what they believed: that only armed resistance could restore the honor of the Jewish people. They had to carry on, even against all odds.

Revolt!

Yitzhak Zuckerman

The organization of an armed uprising in the Warsaw ghetto was assigned to five people: Yitzhak Zuckerman, Zivia Lubetkin, Mordechai Anielewicz, Miriam Heinsdorf, and Israel Kanal. From mid-September on there were daily meetings to develop the structure of the JFO and a strategy for armed revolt.

Zivia was not just an organizer but a full participant in the process of building a fighting force and preparing for battle. Throughout the ghetto she urged the Jews to resist deportation and join the fighters. She filled lightbulbs with sulfur to use as bombs. She set fire to empty stores and warehouses so that the enemy could not make use of them. She also went around to the empty houses of Jews who had been deported and collected valuable items that could be sold on the other side of the ghetto wall. And she went to the Judenrat, the Nazi-controlled Jewish council that governed the ghetto, to demand money for weapons. By the end of 1942, it was the JFO, and not the Judenrat, that exerted the major influence on life in the ghetto.

Slowly but steadily, the JFO increased its strength. But when the Germans again surrounded the ghetto, this time on the evening of January 18, 1943, the commanders were caught without a plan. One JFO unit was swept up in the first round of selection, and most lost their lives quickly. The other units, however, were able to wait under cover for the Germans to attack and then counterattack from their hiding places.

Zivia's unit consisted of forty men and women armed with four hand grenades, four pistols, some iron pipes, heavy sticks, and the sulfur bombs they had invented. Yitzhak Katznelson, a poet and teacher who later died in Auschwitz, raised their spirits that morning with his eloquent words: "We should be happy that we are preparing ourselves, arms in hand, to meet the enemy and die if necessary. Our armed struggle will be an inspiration to future generations."

Zivia waited alone at her post, her heart pounding in the eerie silence. All at once the stillness was shattered, and she could hear the terrible sounds of Jews being rounded up—the angry shouting, the barking dogs, the mournful cries, the screams of terror. Then she heard the stomping boots of the German soldiers moving closer, first entering the building, then climbing the stairs.

The Germans burst into the apartment where a young Jewish man, Zacharia Artstein, sat reading. Suddenly, he leaped up, pulled a pistol, and shot dead two of the attackers. The other Germans scrambled to retreat, and the Jewish fighters sprang into action. In the end they stripped the dead Germans of their weapons and went after those who had fled down the stairs.

When all the Germans were gone, the Jewish fighters were speechless. Something incredible had taken place. They had not expected to remain alive, yet they had killed German soldiers and suffered only one injury. The mighty Germans—conquerors of the world—had retreated in fright from a handful of poorly equipped young Jews.

The group's euphoria did not last, however. When the Germans returned with more troops, Zivia's unit had already left by way of the attic and set out across the rooftops to a building about five blocks away. They traveled silently, in a long line, slowly making their way

Zivia Lubetkin returned to Warsaw in 1940 to help the Jewish youth, such as those pictured opposite, survive the Nazi regime.

up and down, over the icy, snow-covered roofs, four and five stories above the ghetto streets. The treacherous journey ended at 44 Muranowska Street, where they promptly took up positions in the apartments and stairwells.

There was hardly a moment to rest and regain their energy before the Germans arrived, entered the building, and charged up the stairs. But again the young Jewish fighters were quick. As their attackers neared the top of the stairs, they opened fire and hurled a hand grenade down into the entryway. And again the Germans retreated, dragging away their wounded and dead soldiers.

The next day the Germans returned again, and they were met by a shower of bullets that sent them running. When they came back with reinforcements, they found their dead and wounded soldiers stripped of weapons and the Jewish fighters gone.

The January *Aktion* had lasted only four days. The German plan to deport the remaining Jews from the Warsaw ghetto was halted by this unexpected armed resistance. The mood of the fighters was transformed. They were exhausted, physically and mentally, but their lives were filled with new meaning. "Now that we had found the strength to stand up against the murderers," Zivia wrote later, "our deaths too would not be in vain."

With Courage Unparalleled

The startling resistance of the Jews and the headlong retreat of the Germans brought great displeasure to Heinrich Himmler, the Nazi leader who had ordered the *Aktion*. Weeks passed, then months, while the Germans reassessed their strategy and regrouped for the final attack. This time Himmler's order was absolutely clear: the total destruction of the ghetto once and for all, by whatever means necessary.

The JFO knew the Germans would return, and they worked furiously to prepare themselves for the next attack. After the January uprising the Jewish fighters found that they had earned a place of authority in the ghetto. The Judenrat and the Jewish police now feared them while the masses of Jews regarded them as their only hope for the future.

Members of the JFO command executed the head of the Jewish

police to prevent him from turning more Jews over to the Nazis, and they robbed the ghetto bank to obtain money for weapons. When that wasn't enough, they imposed taxes on the rich Jews who remained in the ghetto. The Polish underground finally acknowledged the Jewish resistance, providing one hundred guns and a large quantity of explosives. But it would take millions of Polish zlotys to buy enough arms for the growing number of Jews who were ready to fight.

And so the Jewish youth became the leaders and the defenders of the ghetto. Their kibbutzim became the main bases for the fighting units of the JFO. By mid-April there were twenty-two organized units comprising a fighting force of about five hundred men and women. If there had been more weapons, there would have been more fighters, but the flow had been abruptly cut off.

On the evening of April 18, the JFO contact outside the ghetto walls, Yitzhak Zuckerman, sent word that the confrontation was imminent: German troops were beginning to surround the ghetto. The unit commanders met at 29 Mila Street to distribute weapons and review their plan. Every person with arms was called on to fight. Those women and children who had no weapons were to go down into the bunkers. Their best hope was to try to escape to the Polish side or to the forest during the chaos of the fighting.

Throughout the night Zivia made the rounds of the fighting units in the central ghetto, making sure everyone was ready for battle. At dawn she returned to her own unit and took her place with the frontline fighters near the main gate.

Looking down from her post on the top floor of the corner building at Nalewki and Gesia Streets, Zivia saw that thousands of German soldiers with machine guns were closing in on the ghetto. At 6:00 A.M. the first phalanx marched through the gate, heading right into the minefield that the JFO had planted under the main streets of the ghetto. The explosives were connected to electric currents, and the flick of a switch hurled the marching soldiers into the air. Zivia's unit sent a burst of hand grenades and bombs pouring down on them followed by a shower of bullets.

The Germans kept coming, and Lubetkin's unit battled on for hours. The climax came when the Germans finally got inside the building where the Jewish fighters were based. Zacharia Artstein, the unit commander, quickly reorganized the fighters to barrage the attackers with hand grenades and Molotov cocktails. Again the Germans retreated, leaving their dead behind. But they returned quickly, this time with a caravan of heavy tanks. Again the Jewish fighters showered them with grenades and bombs, and the first tank took a direct hit, exploding in flames.

The Germans withdrew, leaving the Jewish fighters stunned and breathless. Overcome by euphoria, they hugged and kissed one another. "I cannot tell you which emotion was stronger at the moment," Zivia recalled, "the satisfaction of our revenge or the joy of being alive."

Skirmishes continued, and still the fighters held out. On the third night of the uprising, Zivia, who had not closed her eyes for

German troops set fire to the Warsaw ghetto in May 1943 to destroy the Jews once and for all.

days, set out with one of her comrades to check on the units stationed along Mila Street. For three days they had been cut off from the others and had no idea what was happening elsewhere in the ghetto.

Under cover of darkness, they wound their way through back alleys until they reached the bunker that was the base for about one hundred Jewish fighters. There was no hint of activity inside. Lubetkin rapped anxiously on the wall and stated the password, expecting the worst. She was stunned when the door opened to reveal almost everyone safely inside. Her friends in the bunker reported only one Jewish death among all the fighting units on Mila Street. German losses, they told her, had been great. All over the ghetto Jewish fighters had repelled the German attack. Someone turned on the radio, and there was music to match the high spirits of the Jewish fighters. Suddenly, the music stopped, and a voice broke in. The underground Polish radio station reported that the Jews of the Warsaw ghetto had risen in revolt against the Germans. The broadcaster said that the Jews were fighting "with courage unparalleled in history." In all of Europe, it was the first instance of a civilian uprising against the Nazi occupation.

"Tell the World"

Eventually, the Germans destroyed the ghetto, but not in combat. With bombs dropped from the air and flaming torches thrown from all sides, they set the ghetto on fire. They would suffocate the Jews or burn them alive. The ghetto burned for days, then weeks, while life on the other side of the wall went on as usual. At night Poles went up onto their rooftops to watch the spectacle.

On May 8, Zivia made her way through the smoldering rubble to check again on her comrades at 18 Mila Street. What she found this time was a shocking scene: the bodies of more than one hundred Jewish fighters, all victims of a poisonous gas that had been sprayed into their bunker. Lying among the dead was the handsome young commander, Mordechai Anielewicz.

On that terrible night the surviving fighters came together to decide what to do next. The situation was desperate: no food, no water, hardly any arms, and no ammunition for the few guns and pistols they did have. What more, then, could they do?

Someone suggested that a group try to escape through the sewers to the Polish side and see what could be done there. Zivia did not want to leave anyone behind, but those who were too weak for the difficult trek urged the others to go ahead: "Go. Tell the world about our fight. Tell of our loneliness. Tell the world."

About one hundred Jewish fighters plunged into the underground sewers. Some died in the filthy waters; others were killed as

they emerged into the daylight. Zivia was one of the lucky ones who made it onto a truck and into the forest. Three days later, she was reunited with Yitzhak, who had been working frantically on the plan to rescue the fighters from the sewers. More than a year later, in August 1944, Zivia and Yitzhak joined with the Polish partisans in their unsuccessful uprising against the Germans. When the Soviet army liberated Warsaw, in January 1945, they were in hiding in an apartment on the outskirts of the city.

Many of the Nazi officers who were responsible for crimes against humanity were tried and convicted at Nuremberg after the war. Many were executed. Others were imprisoned for life.

At last Zivia and Yitzhak were free to make their way to Palestine, and yet neither of them was ready to leave. They still felt responsible for keeping their movement alive. So Yitzhak stayed on to work in Poland while Zivia spent the next year in Romania, helping other Jewish refugees get to Palestine.

At the end of May 1946, Zivia Lubetkin finally arrived in Palestine. *The Palestine Post* reported that a government delegation went onto her ship to greet the woman known as "the Joan of Arc of Jewish Warsaw." (Joan of Arc, one of the great heroines of European history, had inspired and organized the French to resist the English siege of Orleans in 1429. She, too, had been willing to die for the honor of her people.)

Zivia brought to Palestine the amazing story of the young Jews who fought beyond all odds for the honor of their people. As founding members of Kibbutz Lohamei Haghetaot, a community of former ghetto fighters, and Bet Lohamei Haghetaot, a museum and library,

Zivia Lubetkin and Yitzhak Zuckerman did everything they could to preserve that legacy for future generations. Bet Lohamei Haghetaot has published more than one hundred books about the Holocaust, including Zivia Lubetkin's own memoir, *In the Days of Destruction and Revolt*.

While the uprising in the Warsaw ghetto did not change the outcome of the war, it did set an important example for those who fought the next war in which the fate of the Jews was at stake: the 1948 War of Indepen-dence. And it has been an inspiration to all the soldiers who have since worn the uniform of the Israel Defense Forces.

Zivia Lubetkin and Yitzhak Zuckerman settled on Kibbutz Lohamei Haghetaot, where they lived simply, raised two children, and continued working for their Zionist ideals. Zivia served as head of the Youth and Pioneering Department of the Jewish Agency and as a member of the central committee of Kibbutz Ha-Meuchad, the major association of kibbutzim. She was also an important witness at the trial of Adolf Eichmann, the Nazi officer who was convicted and executed in Jerusalem for his central role in the annihilation of the Jews. Zivia Lubetkin died of cancer in 1978. Today numerous public institutions as well as streets throughout Israel, and a kibbutz in the Galilee, are named in her honor.

Those who died at the hands of the Nazis are remembered in Holocaust museums and monuments in Israel and around the world. Above: A monument to the destroyed communities at Yad Vashem, Jerusalem.

CHAPTER 4

Ida Kaminska
LEADING LADY
(1899–1980)

During the darkest years of the twentieth century, when anti-Semitism and war were tearing Jews apart, a grand and tough-spirited woman named Ida Kaminska presided over a special place where Jews could still come together as Jews and celebrate their common language and heritage. That place was the Yiddish theater, and for more than sixty years Ida Kaminska was its most famous actress. In the towns and villages of pre-

war eastern Europe, a performance by Ida Kaminska and her troupe attracted all sorts of Jews—rich and poor, religious and secular, intellectuals and ordinary folk—as if she held a magnet to their souls. On the stage she played all types of roles—tragic and comic, musical and fanciful—but her struggle for the survival of the theater she loved was perhaps her most amazing performance of all.

*I*t was Academy Awards night in Hollywood. The audience of glittering celebrities grew quiet as the presenter read out the list of nominees for best performance by an actress in a leading role. There were the Redgrave sisters, Lynn and Vanessa, from the distinguished family of British actors; Anouk Aimée, a romantic French actress; and Elizabeth Taylor, America's glamorous screen idol. And there was Ida Kaminska, a white-haired lady from Poland who had stepped out of the Yiddish theater into her first film role.

Ida Kaminska had been recruited by two directors from Czechoslovakia for the lead role in *The Shop on Main Street,* a film with an explicit Jewish theme. This powerful story of the Holocaust had received the Oscar for the best foreign film of 1966, and Ida Kaminska had been nominated the following year for her performance in the film as the Jewish shopkeeper, Mrs. Lautmann, an elderly widow who cannot comprehend what is happening to the Jews of her town in Poland.

The Oscar for best actress went, as expected, to Elizabeth Taylor, but Ida Kaminska was not disappointed. To her the nomination itself was the prize. It was a tribute to a cultural tradition that could have died in the gas chambers of Auschwitz, and it was a sweet reward for her lifelong efforts to keep that tradition alive.

The Kaminska Magic

The name Kaminska may have been new to Hollywood, but audiences throughout Europe had been applauding the

Kaminski dynasty for decades. Ida's father, Abraham Isaac Kaminski, founded the first Yiddish theater in Warsaw in 1887, when he was twenty years old. Ida's mother, the legendary Esther Rachel Kaminska, was its shining star, enthralling audiences wherever the troupe toured.

Ida Kaminska made her own stage debut at the age of five, and throughout her youth she performed in the towns and villages of eastern Europe. After her father's death, in 1918, and her mother's death, in 1925, Ida took over the company and starred in most of its productions. She played the great female roles that had made her mother famous and added many new ones to the repertoire.

Like her mother, Ida toured widely and became one of the most popular "leading ladies" of Europe. There was a saying in the theater world that captured the effect she had on audiences: "Falling in love with Ida is as inevitable as the measles. One case is mild, another more severe, but everyone succumbs."

Ida Kaminska's fame and popularity helped her get through the terrible years of World War II. When the Nazis entered Poland, admirers of the great actress were eager to help her escape. Along with the other members of her immediate family—her husband, Meir Melman; her daughter, Ruth Kaminska-Turkow; and her son-in-law, Addy Rosner—she was smuggled across the border into the relative safety of Soviet territory.

For two years the family traveled eastward. Seeking refuge from war and pogroms, they went from Lemno to Rovno to Kharkov to Baku. Finally, in October 1941, they found a safe haven in Frunze, a town in Soviet Central Asia. And it was just in time. Only a few weeks later Kaminska gave birth to her son, Viktor, and a few weeks after that Ruth's daughter, Erika, was born.

Frunze was an exotic Asian town with fewer than one hundred Jewish residents, but the number grew steadily as more Jewish refugees poured in from the west and the north. Among them were many artists and writers, who were thrilled to learn that Ida Kaminska was there, too. They looked to her to organize a Yiddish theater right there in central Asia.

Kaminska didn't have a single script with her, but she wrote down half a dozen plays from memory, assembled a group of actors, and rented a small theater, where they began to perform. She understood how much it meant to the refugees to come together as Jews and hear the comforting sound of their beloved Yiddish language.

For more than two years Kaminska held a troupe of actors together, and the audiences kept coming. She gave them what they needed: tragedy to help them express and share their sorrows, comedy that enabled them to laugh at their misfortunes, nostalgic journeys, flights of the imagination, and above all, affirmation of their heritage.

Some of the town's permanent residents attended the performances as well, but rumblings against the Jews were always in the air. By 1944 the Kaminska clan decided it was time to move on to Moscow, the Soviet capital, which had a large Jewish population. In Moscow there would be bigger audiences and greater camaraderie. Or so they thought.

Ida Kaminska was welcomed warmly by the community of Jewish artists and writers in Moscow—after all, she was the most famous Jewish actress in the world. Yet for two years she was never given the opportunity to perform. When an invitation finally came, in 1946, she accepted

Ida Kaminska with her mother Esther, around 1907. Ida Kaminska made her stage debut at the age of five and, like her mother before her, became a star of Yiddish theater.

gratefully. Then she was told that the performance must be in Polish, not in Yiddish, the language with which she was identified.

Kaminska was outraged by this insult, and she did not disguise her feelings. "What?" she snapped. "I'm known as a Yiddish actress. Why should I perform in Polish in Moscow?" A few days later the performance was canceled. With anti-Semitism on the rise in Moscow too, it would be a long wait before she could appear on stage again on her own cultural terms.

Return to Poland

When the nightmare of World War II was finally over, Ida Kaminska couldn't wait to get back to Poland. She knew all about the terrible destruction of the Warsaw ghetto. And she had heard the shocking news of a recent pogrom that killed fifty Jews in the Polish town of Kielce. But still she felt that her first destination had to be Poland, the place where the Yiddish theater was born and had flourished for so many years.

Most of the Jews who survived the Holocaust made their way to America, Israel, or Western Europe. But many stayed in the Soviet Union, and even more surprisingly, about forty-five thousand Jews were ready to begin life again in Poland. Many of them, like Ida Kaminska and her husband, had a strong sense of Jewish continuity and a great love of Yiddish culture. Poland had been the center of Jewish life before the war, a vibrant community of three million, and these Jews who wished to return had a deep longing to rebuild what they had lost.

From any reasonable point of view, a revival of Jewish life in Poland was unlikely. Arriving in Warsaw in November 1946, Kaminska and Melman found destruction that was far greater than anything they'd ever imagined. Most of the city, it seemed, was buried under heaps of rubble. Kaminska described the ghetto as "a desert of dust, stones, bricks, and sand." Only one Jewish cemetery remained.

Kaminska felt that she had come to the grave of the entire Jewish people. At her mother's tombstone she collapsed onto the ground and wept. Suddenly it all seemed crazy. "What is the point of going on with this?" she asked herself. "What can I possibly accomplish here?" But the feeling of her mother's spiritual presence renewed her strength. She wasn't ready to give up. Never one to be governed by so-called common sense, she resolved to keep the legacy alive—for herself, for her mother, and for her people.

Revival in the Ruins

Ida Kaminska longed to perform again in Warsaw, but no trace of its once glorious Yiddish theater remained. Now there were only

*Opposite:
Ida Kaminska as
a young actress
in Poland before
World War II.*

two Yiddish theaters left in Poland, one in Wroclaw and one in Lodz. The Polish Ministry of Culture, eager to appear friendly to the Jews, appointed Kaminska to go to Lodz and organize the troupe there. For the time being, it was the best thing she could do.

The Yiddish theater of Lodz had been destroyed by the Germans. When Kaminska and Melman arrived, the remnants of the troupe were housed in a primitive little building that was barely usable. Kaminska, Melman, and a group of local Jews soon persuaded the municipal authorities to help reconstruct the original theater. In

the meantime, with contributions from two generous American Jews and from the remaining Jewish community of Lodz, Kaminska and her troupe set out to fix up the ramshackle building for temporary use.

The task of renovation took many months. Finally, in 1948, the Yiddish theater of Lodz was proud to open its doors again. It did so with a fine performance of *Glückel of Hameln Demands Justice*. The play, about a Jewish woman who speaks out against oppression, was a courageous choice. Although it was set in Germany in the seventeenth century, its relevance to Nazism and Communism could not go unnoticed.

Ida Kaminska knew that things were better for Jews in Poland than they were in the Soviet Union, where Jewish artists and intellectuals were beginning to disappear into prisons and labor camps. By 1949, all the Yiddish theaters in the Soviet Union were dead, along with most other forms of Jewish culture. In Poland, however, Jewish culture was beginning to thrive again.

In 1949, the Yiddish theater was brought under the direct sponsorship of the Polish government. This "nationalization" of the theater meant that the government could keep a closer watch over the political content of the plays that were produced and could more easily censor what it considered objectionable. But it also assured the company of the financial support it needed to survive. As part of the nationalization, the government wanted the two Yiddish

In the years before World War II, Warsaw, the capital of Poland, was a great center of arts, learning, and commerce for Jews and non-Jews alike.

theaters to be brought together in Lodz, with Meir Melman as administrative director and Ida Kaminska as artistic director. Before long, however, the government determined that the theater should be moved to Wroclaw, an area where there were supposedly more Jews. In Wroclaw, Melman was replaced by an administrator who was closer to the Communist party. Kaminska, however, was asked to stay on as the artistic director.

These changes made Ida Kaminska uneasy, but she resolved to tolerate them. Most important to her was the ability to continue her work—and eventually to return to Warsaw. She believed that more Jews would be returning to Poland's capital city. And she was convinced that the company's artistry would be at its best if the company were back in the city with the greatest tradition of Yiddish theater in the world.

There was a more recent historical legacy to consider as well: "A Yiddish theater in Poland," Kaminska wrote in her autobiography, "had to be in the city where Jews were martyred and where, in the Warsaw Ghetto Uprising, they displayed their greatest heroism."

Ida Kaminska frequently traveled to Warsaw to exert pressure on government officials. Finally, in 1954, the Ministry of Culture agreed to her request, and the Yiddish State Theater came home to Warsaw. In December 1955, on the thirtieth anniversary of her mother's death, it was officially renamed the Esther Rachel Kaminska Yiddish State Theater. With all the synagogues either destroyed or shut down, the theater was the only place in Warsaw where a Jewish soul could still breathe.

Many Poles were not pleased with the government's support of the Yiddish theater or with the theater's prestigious location in the former Theater of the Polish Army. But many others attended the performances, using special headsets that provided simultaneous translation into Polish. Some considered it their moral duty to support Jewish culture because the Jews had suffered so much on Polish soil. And from the government's point of view, a showcase for Jewish culture was a credit to Polish Communism. Wherever the Yiddish theater troupe traveled, it enhanced Poland's image in the world.

Although her theater was based in Poland and was supported by the Polish government, Ida Kaminska always viewed it as a theater for world Jewry. Over the years her view proved correct as invitations poured in from theaters around the world. In 1956, the company performed in Paris and Antwerp. The next year it traveled to London and Amsterdam. Later it visited South America, Australia, the United States, and Germany. The troupe performed for Jews and non-Jews, commoners and royalty. Wherever it went, whatever the play—whether a folk tale by Shalom Aleichem or a contemporary drama by Arthur Miller—the performance was in Yiddish.

A New Anti-Semitism

Ida Kaminska was a great stage presence, and she was adored wherever she performed. But in all the company's travels nothing moved her more than the warm reception she received in Israel in 1957. It was her first visit to Israel, with eleven special solo performances scheduled over the course of six weeks. One of her biggest fans was Golda Meir, who was then Israel's foreign minister. On opening night Golda Meir came backstage after the performance, embraced Kaminska, and exclaimed, "What can I tell you? I love you!"

The Israeli public was so enthusiastic that Kaminska considered bringing her theater to Israel. But after discussion and reflection she concluded that the company could reach more people if it kept its base in Warsaw and toured Israel for several weeks each year. Perhaps Kaminska also understood the limited appeal of Yiddish culture in Israel, with its strong commitment to the modern Hebrew language.

Jews flocked to the Yiddish theater in America as well as in Europe. In America, audiences adored the Yiddish actress Molly Picon for her expressive acting and impish personality.

PALACE THEATRE

STRAUSS STREET   Near Pitkin Avenue
Telephone HY 5-8382

"FARBLONDJETE HONEYMOON"

א פארבלאנדזשעטער האניטון

Although Ida Kaminska was determined to stay in Poland, by the late 1950s many of her actors were ready to leave. When tighter control of the government by Soviet-backed Communists created new waves of anti-Semitism, some fifteen thousand Jews—about one-third of Poland's Jewish population—decided to emigrate. Among them were about half the players of the Yiddish State Theater, most of whom went to Israel.

Permission to emigrate required the formal consent of a supervisor. For the actors of the Yiddish State Theater, that person was Ida Kaminska—and she never stopped anyone from leaving. She understood that every Jew had to make his or her own choice. Losing so many members was a crisis for the company, but Kaminska and Melman endured, hiring and training new actors to replace those who left.

A more serious crisis erupted in 1967, when Israel went to war with its Arab neighbors. The Polish people seemed to sympathize with the Israelis, but the Polish government did not. On the second day of the war, the government expelled the Israeli ambassador and cut off diplomatic relations with Israel. It was the beginning of a new brand of anti-Semitism, called anti-Zionism. And it was not silent.

On June 19, Wladyslaw Gomulka, secretary general of Poland's Communist Party, issued a public statement that made things very

New York's Grand Theater was a favorite place for Jewish immigrants to see Yiddish plays. Unlike Yiddish theaters in Russia and Poland, where Kaminska performed, those established in America were never closed by hostile government forces.

Ida Kaminska stars in the play Mirele Efros *in 1968. Larger than life characters with exaggerated gestures were typical of the Yiddish theater genre—whether in comedy or drama.*

clear for the the Jews: "Poland will not tolerate in its midst a fifth column." Everyone understood that the "fifth column"—the implied traitors—were the Jews. And in a later speech Gomulka declared that "whoever doesn't like it here can leave."

Gomulka's "fifth column" speech was delivered on the date that had been set for Ida Kaminska's jubilee, a celebration of her many decades in the Yiddish theater. The celebration was postponed because of the intense anti-Israel feeling that followed the Six-Day War. When it finally took place, on September 18, it was a rare opportunity for Polish Jews to come together and demonstrate their continuing attachment to Jewish culture. Also in attendance were the most prominent representatives of the Polish theater and officials from the Ministry of Culture. On the program that evening were scenes from some of Kaminska's best-loved plays and a preview of

Ida Kaminska and Her Theater, a film that was never again shown in Poland. After the program, the honoree was led to a throne at center stage and showered with flowers, gifts, and praise.

The joyous mood snapped, however, when the Polish vice minister of culture refered to Israel as the "aggressor" in the Middle East. Speakers from the Polish theater world and from the Jewish community chose to ignore it, but Kaminska would not. When her turn came, she delivered the remarks she had prepared for the occasion, then added a special message for the Jews in the audience: "Not everything that I wanted to say can be said now, but in these fateful hours for the Jewish people you feel what I feel, and even if I say little, you will understand much." Her words drew stormy applause from the Jews and, later, some quiet congratulations from non-Jews.

The Jews could not hold out against the vigorous anti-Israel campaign. Eventually, the Polish government succeeded in forcing representatives of the country's Jewish organizations to sign a public statement condemning Israel. The government was shrewd enough, however, to stay away from Kaminska, who had shown herself to be a tough opponent. The Polish Communists seemed to understand that she would not pay their price for the government's support. If she refused to sign their statement, they could not expel her or put her in prison—she was too famous for that. For the time being, they left her alone.

A Question of Honor

In the spring of 1968, Kaminska, Melman, and their ensemble left Poland temporarily for their long-awaited debut in New York, the city with the largest Jewish population in the world. It was a triumph! For more than two months audiences packed a Broadway theater for performances of *Mirele Efros*, a Yiddish-theater classic by Jacob Gordin, and *Mother Courage*, a contemporary drama by the German playwright Bertolt Brecht. Each day hundreds of fans gathered outside the theater and pleaded, "Don't go back to Poland. Stay with us."

Was there really an American audience for high-quality Yiddish theater? It seemed so, but Ida Kaminska still was not ready to make a change. To her American admirers she explained that she and her family did not want to be runaways, that it was a question of honor.

"We'll return to Poland," she told them, "and then we'll see what will be."

What they saw was a dramatic rise in anti-Semitism. From the day they arrived in Warsaw, they felt like strangers. Doors were shutting all around them. All over Poland theaters that used to welcome the Kaminska troupe were suddenly not available. Requests to tour abroad were not approved by the government. And the construction of a new Yiddish theater, begun two years earlier with funds provided by an international Jewish organization, came to a halt.

When the Jewish Culture Committee in Warsaw refused to complain to the authorities, Kaminska decided that she would go on her own to one of her superiors in the Ministry of Culture. He was a kind man whom she had always trusted, and this time he responded to her with tears in his eyes: "It's bad for you," he said quietly. "I don't mean just you personally or your theater—I mean all of you!"

Golda Meir was one of Ida Kaminska's biggest fans. Here she greets the actress backstage after a performance in Israel in 1957. Also pictured are Ida Kaminska's husband, Meir Melman, and her daughter, Ruth Kaminska-Turkow.

At that moment Kaminska knew what she had been dreading for years: There was no future for Jewish life in Communist Poland. The Jewish population had already dwindled to twenty-five thousand. With more young Jews fleeing anti-Semitism and more old ones dying, the culture she had fought to preserve was destined to fade away. It was no longer in the Polish government's interest to keep it alive.

Ida Kaminska could have simply retired and collected the pension to which she was entitled, but she would not stay in a country that had betrayed her and her people. What's more, she wanted to go on with the work she loved. To Jews all over the world she had always brought an important message: "We're here and doing everything in our power to continue to exist." To begin again in a new country would be difficult at her age—she was nearly seventy—but she was determined to try.

Ida Kaminska and her family left Poland in July 1968. Kaminska thought they would first try America, where she had been offered a film role, stage appearances, and a book contract. While waiting in Vienna for the travel arrangements and the necessary documents to allow them to enter the United States, they gladly accepted Israel's invitation to come for another visit.

Kaminska did not anticipate that she would perform in Israel this time, but once she arrived, the requests for *Mirele Efros* did not cease. Finally, in August 1968, the play was performed in Jerusalem with Kaminska, Melman, and Ruth Kaminska-Turkow in the leading roles and an ensemble of Israeli actors playing the supporting parts.

When the final curtain went down, Zalman Shazar, the president of Israel, came backstage to Kaminska's dressing room with a message that meant the world to her: "If you want to stay here we will take you with open arms; if you have to go, go in good health, life, and peace, and do your work for the Jews, for all of us. May our blessings go with you."

Ida Kaminska settled in the United States, where she appeared in another film, The Angel Levine, *in 1970 and published her autobiography,* My Life, My Theater, *in 1973. But she did not find a sizable audience or adequate financial support for a Yiddish art theater. In 1974, she and Meir Melman moved to Israel to join a newly formed but short-lived Yiddish theater in Tel Aviv. Ida Kaminska died in New York in 1980, still remembered for her indomitable spirit and her glorious contribution to Jewish culture.*

CHAPTER 5

Ida Nudel
GUARDIAN ANGEL
(1931–)

*I*da Nudel was born fourteen years after the revolution
that brought the Communists to power in Russia and created
a new country, the Soviet Union. Her parents, Chaya
Filanovsky and Yakov Nudel, were optimistic about their
future under Communism, and they raised their children to be
good Soviet citizens. Like so many other Russian Jews, they
believed the Communists' promise of a society in which political
power would at last belong to the people.

As it turned out, however, power in the Soviet Union was tightly held by the leaders of the Communist Party, and punishment came quickly to any citizen who dared question their policies. Censorship was the norm. There was no freedom to speak out, to travel to another country, to choose a place to live, or to practice a religion. As a result, more than two million Jews eventually lost touch with Judaism and with the rest of the Jewish world. It was Israel's victory in the 1967 Six-Day War that awakened the Jews of the Soviet Union, arousing their pride and a concern about being Jewish. Out of those feelings the movement for Soviet Jewry was born, and Ida Nudel emerged as a voice of her people.

One evening in June 1970, Ida Nudel returned from her job as an economist at the Moscow Planning Institute and climbed the stairs to her small apartment. Ever since her sister, Lena, had given her a short-wave radio as a birthday present, she had something special to look forward to. Most nights, if she jiggled the knob patiently, she could pick up a news broadcast on the Voice of America, the BBC (British Broadcasting Corporation) World Service, or sometimes even Kol Israel ("the Voice of Israel"). Since June 1967, when Israel defeated the Arab armies in the Six-Day War, Soviet broadcasts had been filled with condemnations of Israel and with the most unlikely stories about what was going on there. The short-wave radio was Ida Nudel's link to reality.

That night Ida was lucky enough to pick up the Voice of Israel, and what she heard seemed utterly fantastic: A group of Soviet Jews, assisted by two non-Jewish Russians, had attempted to hijack a small Soviet plane at the Leningrad airport and commandeer it to Israel. Their courageous mission was halted by the Soviet military police, and the hijackers were sent to prison to await trial. But they had made a dramatic statement that was heard around the world.

The news changed her life. "Others are doing something," she said to herself, "but what about me?" Ever since the Six-Day War she had felt a restless longing, but she hadn't known where to turn. If something was happening, if something could be done for the Soviet Jews, she wanted to be part of it.

Ida Nudel spoke with a few people she could trust. One person sent her to another, and eventually she received the telephone number of a Jew named Vladimir Prestin, who was secretly teaching Hebrew to other Jews. She made the call, and Prestin immediately understood what she wanted. "Come over," he said warmly. When she entered his apartment that evening, her entire life took on new meaning and direction: She had entered the world of the Jewish emigration movement.

Most of Ida Nudel's new friends in the emigration movement were "refuseniks," Jews who had petitioned the Soviet government for visas that would allow them to emigrate to Israel and had been refused. Once their desire to emigrate was known, they became outcasts in Soviet society. Refuseniks were routinely fired from their jobs, expelled from institutions of higher learning, and shunned by their neighbors. Their telephone lines were tapped and even disconnected. Their mail was censored and often confiscated.

The Soviet secret police, the notorious KGB, kept a close watch on the refuseniks. KGB agents would enter an apartment without warning to break up a group that had gathered to study Hebrew or to celebrate a Jewish holiday. They waited outside refuseniks' apartments, followed them everywhere, roughed them up, and made arrests on false charges. Some refuseniks were sentenced to prison or to forced-labor camps in Siberia for claiming the right to live among their own people.

These were the risks of requesting a visa and participating in the Jewish emigration movement. Yet the number of applicants grew steadily. By the end of the summer of 1971, Ida Nudel, too, had assembled the necessary documents and joined their ranks. In January 1972, she was called to the government visa office and abruptly informed that her application had been denied. The reason: "national security."

"But how can that be?" Ida protested. "What government secrets could I possibly have?" The officer replied that in her work at the Moscow Planning Institute she might have overheard something secret that could be shared with enemies of the Soviet Union. "It is therefore in our interest to keep you here," he stated firmly. She dared to ask for how long and was stunned by his answer: "Five or six years."

The refusal was all the more upsetting because it meant a long separation from her sister, brother-in-law, and five-year-old nephew, who recently had received visas. Ida urged them to leave without her. Sad as they were, they all knew that an opportunity for freedom could not be forfeited.

It was a difficult good-bye. No one could say when the family would be reunited, and they knew that Ida would be alone in the Soviet Union. Her parents were dead, and she was not married; her only family would be in Israel, which was practically another world. In addition, she had been fired from her job, with no income to count on.

Yet in spite of her fear and uncertainty, Ida Nudel was able to see a positive side to her situation. Because she did not have a regular job, she would have more time to work for the emigration movement. And because she was alone, she would not have to worry that the government might punish her family for her activities. Ida was trapped, but she also had a sudden and exciting sense of freedom. She was free to do whatever needed to be done for her people.

Prisoners of Zion

Soon other Jews in the Soviet Union began turning to Ida Nudel. That summer of 1972, for example, she was ready to help a refusenik named Greta Markman, who had come to Moscow to find a lawyer for her husband. Vladimir Markman had been arrested for "slander against the Soviet system." Not surprisingly, Greta could not find anyone willing to take on the defense of a Jewish activist.

Ida Nudel proposed that a hunger strike be held at the central office of the Communist Party of the Soviet Union to protest the denial of Vladimir Markman's legal rights. The strike began with two people and grew to eleven. For four days the participants resisted orders to leave and threats of arrest. Finally, on the morning of the fifth day, the police blocked their entry and put an end to the strike. The protesters hoped, however, that they had made their point.

Did hunger strikes accomplish anything? Sometimes it was hard

to see the immediate results, but they were part of an overall strategy:
The refuseniks would do whatever they could to bring their situation
to the public, and especially to the attention of reporters, diplomats,
and other visitors from the West. They wanted Soviet leaders to
believe that their actions were being watched, in their own country
and abroad.

The strategy depended on an information network in which
Nudel's friend Vladimir Prestin played a central role. Day and night
Prestin received calls from all over the Soviet Union with news
about refuseniks, Jewish prisoners, and their families. He in turn
dispensed the information to supporters outside the Soviet Union.
When the KGB tried to subvert the network by disconnecting
Prestin's telephone, Nudel was ready to step in and take over his
responsibilities.

Once again Ida Nudel's life underwent a dramatic change. Now
her own little apartment became central headquarters for information about refuseniks: job losses, threats, arrests, and any other kind
of cruel treatment they suffered. Any time at all someone might
telephone or appear at her door with important news or a request
for help.

As the number of refuseniks grew, so did the number of Jewish
political prisoners, the "Prisoners of Zion." These courageous individuals
had been imprisoned on false charges—such as "anti-Soviet activity"
or "malicious hooliganism"—because of their activities on behalf of
Jewish rights. They were the ones who suffered the most, and Ida
Nudel believed that much more should be done to help them. It was
dangerous for a refusenik to become involved with prisoners, but
she was convinced that someone had to concentrate on their needs.
No one, it seemed, was in a better position than she.

Ida Nudel began her self-appointed task by drawing up a list of
all the Jews who were serving sentences in prisons or labor camps.
With the help of Moisey Mendelevich, whose son Iosif had been
one of the Leningrad hijackers, she discovered Jewish prisoners who
had virtually vanished into thin air. Between 1972 and 1975, there
were forty-six names on her list, many more Jewish prisoners than
anyone had previously realized.

Nudel recorded the names of the prisoners' relatives, their
birthdays, their medical problems, and their other special needs.

Then she found ways to spread this information to other Soviet Jews and to activists in the West. Because of her efforts, people all over the world got to know about the Prisoners of Zion—who they were and what was happening to them. She spoke for people who had been silenced, people she had never met, and through her their voices were heard.

Nudel also corresponded with the prisoners, every one of them, and she did so without the benefit of a computer or a photocopy machine. To convey information of Jewish interest without arousing the censors' suspicions, she copied into the body of her letters news items about Israel, information from the Jewish calendar, or some words of Hebrew greeting in the letters of the Russian alphabet. On the prisoners' birthdays and on holidays, she sent them telegrams signed by more than one hundred Soviet Jewish activists. She had, of course, collected the signatures herself.

The prisoners were amazed by the deeds of this total stranger. To Jews inside the Soviet Union and to their supporters abroad, Ida

A military parade in front of the Kremlin. During seventy years of Communist rule, an oppressive military régime controlled the lives of Soviet citizens.

Nudel became known as the "guardian angel" of the Prisoners of Zion. She would not let anyone forget their suffering. Because of her, other refuseniks felt an obligation to help the prisoners as well. Former refusenik Anatoly (Natan) Sharansky recalls that Ida Nudel was constantly reminding them of those in the camps and prisons, whose situation was even more desperate than theirs.

Nudel spread the word about many special items the prisoners needed to help them survive their ordeal, and visitors from all over the world filled her requests. Always at the top of her list were vitamins that looked like candy, to supplement the pitiful prison diet; high-energy bars of white chocolate; and warm outer clothing to help them endure the bitter, subzero winters. Cigarettes, pens, and three-dimensional postcards were hot items because they could be given to prison guards in return for small favors.

Nudel often prepared packages for the prisoners' relatives to take along on their visits. Many of them turned to her for advice on what to do and say once they arrived at the prison. Afterward they contacted her with the latest information concerning their imprisoned relative's situation. Sometimes the family just left the visit entirely to Nudel and she made the trip by herself.

"Where Is He?"

A face-to-face meeting was the best way to find out what was happening to a prisoner. But prison visits were strictly limited, and most of the labor camps were located in remote parts of the Soviet Union. So Ida Nudel developed an alternative system for keeping track of her prisoners. She set up a writing schedule for each one to follow, and when a card or a letter did not arrive on time, Nudel was ready to react. She immediately sent a telegram or placed a telephone call to the head of the prison to ask what was wrong. "Where is he?" she would demand of the official. "Is he sick? Have you killed him?"

Ida Nudel also sent out alerts to Soviet Jewry watchers abroad. Sometimes her messages were entrusted to tourists she met outside the synagogue on Arkhipova Street, but mostly she relied on Michael Sherbourne, a Russian-speaking British Jew who called her every week from London for an update. The news spread quickly to other activists in England, the United States, and Israel, and a wave of protests came lashing back at the Soviet government.

One example of Nudel's tactics at work can be seen in the case of Simyon Marinov, who was serving a five-year term in a forced-labor camp. After a severe beating by Soviet police, Marinov had been arrested and sentenced on charges of hooliganism, then arrested again. He was brought to his second trial on a stretcher, unable to stand, his body covered with welts.

Ida Nudel did everything possible to tell the world about this man, who was suffering enormously. Activists in the West received regular updates on his condition while Soviet officials were bombarded by inquiries and complaints. Still the beatings went on. Word came that Marinov would soon die if nothing was done for him.

Finally, Nudel came up with a new angle. The Soviets liked to say that their medical care was the most humane in the world, but Marinov's poor health surely contradicted this claim. So she marched

Throughout the 1970s and 1980s, Jews around the world staged demonstrations and other campaigns to publicize the plight of persecuted Jews in the Soviet Union and the Arab world.

Avital Sharansky received an exit visa in 1974, twelve years before her husband, Natan, was allowed to leave. While Ida Nudel continued her work for Sharansky and the other Jewish prisoners from her exile in Siberia, Avital led an international campaign from Israel.

directly to the Moscow office of the director of medicine for the prison camps and let him know what was at stake: If Marinov died, the world would know that the Soviet medical system was to blame.

The threat worked. The director promptly called the head of the camp, demanding a report on Marinov's health. Two days later he informed Nudel that Marinov's life was no longer in danger. The camp officials knew that they would have to answer to their superior in Moscow for their treatment of this prisoner.

Another example of Nudel's intervention is the case of Arieh Hanoch, who had been transferred from prison to a forced-labor camp and was suffering from a serious stomach disorder. For more than a year he received no medical attention, but after Nudel began pestering the Ministry of Health, Hanoch was taken to a doctor and given a more suitable diet.

Another Jewish prisoner, Shimon Grilius, was in terrible pain from a dislocated shoulder, but the prison doctor refused to treat him—until Ida Nudel found out and started complaining. When Grilius finally was released, he appeared twelve hours later at Nudel's apartment, still in his prison uniform. She was waiting for him with a new suit of clothes and "one of her famous liberation meals."

"It was natural to go straight to Ida," said a former prisoner, David Chernoglaz, because "she was the one person above all others who helped to keep up our morale and who constantly helped with letters and parcels, at great risk to herself. . . . All of us prisoners," he said, "considered her a superhuman angel."

Nudel rejoiced when prisoners were released—Marinov, Grilius, Chernoglaz, and all the others who came through Moscow with the long-awaited visa in hand. Each time, she had the deep satisfaction of seeing that her efforts had helped another person survive.

About her own predicament she felt weary and discouraged. The more she made a nuisance of herself, the slimmer were her own chances of getting a visa anytime soon. Officials had warned her to sit quietly and wait if she ever wanted to get out of the Soviet Union. But instead of lying low, she became even bolder.

Ugly Warnings

In December 1974, Ida Nudel was part of a group of thirty refuseniks who staged another hunger strike, this time at the central telegraph office on one of Moscow's busiest streets. The protesters arrived early one morning and sent off telegrams to Soviet officials, demanding the release of all the Prisoners of Zion and the enactment of a fair emigration law. Then they settled in to wait for an answer.

Throughout the day people came in and out of the telegraph office, but the government was silent. Late that night, however, after the volume of business had slowed, the KGB arrived on the scene. The protesters agreed to disperse, but they were led onto waiting buses and delivered to the police. They had broken no law, but they would be punished.

The charge was "hooliganism," stirring up trouble. Ida Nudel's sentence was fifteen days—a short time compared with that given the Prisoners of Zion, but even fifteen days in a Soviet prison was a terrible ordeal. Around the clock Nudel and another woman in the group were locked in a tiny cell. Their daily rations were a piece of dry bread and a cup of lukewarm water—on alternate days a bowl of slops as well. Hungry as they were, the two women had to force themselves to eat. All night long a bright bulb burned in their cell, so they could never escape the eyes of the guards. They lay on hard wooden planks that bruised their bodies, and it was impossible for them to warm themselves.

On the fifteenth day Nudel waited nervously to see whether they would really let her go. It was late in the afternoon when a guard unlocked her cell and led her through a maze of hallways and numbered doors to a small room where she would learn her fate. "Sign here," a uniformed officer ordered gruffly. He shoved a paper and pen into her hands; it was the form authorizing her release.

Ida Nudel was ecstatic to be in her own little apartment once again. It felt like a palace to her, with its clean bed, hot water, books, music, and edible food. Best of all, there were no guards watching her every move. She climbed into bed, turned off her light, and passed the night in peaceful darkness. Not until the next morning did she notice the hole in her ceiling. It was the unmistakable sign of the KGB at work with one of its notorious "bugs." The hole in the ceiling declared that the KGB would never leave her alone. Its agents were everywhere—waiting outside her apartment, tailing her in the street, and now listening through her ceiling. And still she resolved to go about her business as if they didn't exist.

Before long Ida Nudel was planning another demonstration. This time it was on behalf of Silva Zalmanson, the only woman among the Prisoners of Zion. Zalmanson was serving a ten-year sentence for her participation in the attempted Leningrad plane hijacking. When her father reported that she was losing her hearing under the severe conditions of her imprisonment, a group of activists decided to go to the Presidium of the Supreme Soviet and demand Zalmanson's release.

On the night before the designated day, KGB agents knocked on Ida Nudel's door. Somehow they had found out about the plan, and they warned her that she would be arrested if she went ahead with it. The next morning she called their bluff and was on her way to Gorky Street when two thugs cornered her. They jumped her, pinned her down, dragged her off to a police station, and charged her with planning to disturb the public order.

Nudel was forced to submit to a humiliating strip search. Then she was taken to a small, dark cell that contained nothing but a wooden plank on which to sleep. She never knew whether it was day or night or even how many days had passed. She didn't know where she was or how long her punishment would last. When she was finally released, she stopped a stranger on the street to ask what day it was. Saturday, he told her, and she went directly to the synagogue on Arkhipova Street, the one place where Jews could go and meet each other as Jews. Nudel's friends were greatly relieved to see her. They told her that twenty others had been kidnapped on their way to the demonstration. All of them had been held for a week, while an international peace conference was taking place in Moscow. The KGB had wanted to make sure that no public protests would interrupt the proceedings.

Natan Sharansky was convicted of treason for allegedly giving Soviet secrets to the U.S. Central Intelligence Agency, the CIA. Ida Nudel's constant support helped Sharansky endure his nine years of prison and hard labor.

Enemies of the State

Eventually, the KGB let loose with an all-out campaign against the refuseniks, calling them a community of traitors and spies. Shock waves spread when *Izvestiya*, a government-controlled newspaper, published a so-called confession by a Jewish informer named Aleksandr (Sanya) Lipavsky. Lipavsky claimed that certain refuseniks, among them Nudel's friend Anatoly Sharansky, were selling secrets to the U.S. Central Intelligence Agency as part of a worldwide "Zionist conspiracy."

Ida Nudel was not one of those named, but she had no doubt that she was in the same boat. In fact, she had barely finished reading the article when the police pounded on her door. Seven men burst inside, flashed a search warrant, and proceeded to ransack her apartment. Into their sacks they dumped her books and journals, her letters from prisoners and supporters abroad, and her pictures and letters from Israel. Would they arrest her? Not now, she prayed.

"Stop your anti-Soviet activity or we'll put a stop to it ourselves," the chief agent shouted as the men hauled away her most valued possessions. He slammed the door behind them and left her alone, shaking.

Later Nudel learned the terrible news that Anatoly Sharansky had been arrested. Still she didn't give in to the threats. She kept up her work for the prisoners, knowing that each day could be the day of her own arrest.

Meanwhile any opportunity for worldwide attention could not be overlooked. One such occasion was June 1, 1978, the day the United Nations designated for worldwide recognition of the rights

of children. Ida Nudel and some of her friends decided to use that day to call attention to the children and families of the Jewish prisoners and refuseniks. The plan was for small groups of women and children to gather in five diffe-rent Moscow apartments and, at the appointed time, display messages of protest from their windows. Nudel would be alone in her apartment because she knew the KGB would follow her wherever she went or become suspicious of anyone who came to her. She prepared her own placard and got a roll of wallpaper to write on as well.

On the afternoon of June 1, Nudel was ready as planned. But when she looked out her window she froze at the sight of television cameras, a bulldozer, and a crowd of strangers looking up at her apartment. Someone had informed the KGB. She could see the agents stationed on the edges of the crowd and on her neighbor's balcony, just above.

Panicky thoughts raced through her head. Maybe she shouldn't go through with this.

But if they scared her off this time, they would make it harder for her to act in the future. She resolved to go on with the plan. At 5:59 P.M. she opened her window wide and displayed a bold message in enormous letters: KGB, GIVE ME A VISA TO ISRAEL!

What followed was a terrible scene. The agents on the balcony above tore down the sign with metal rods, then smashed her window with a heavy wrench swung from the end of a rope. The crowd below cheered, and someone cried out, "Hitler should have finished the job!" Nudel's only weapon was a bucket of water, which she poured down onto the jeering spectators.

Finally, the crowd dispersed, and Nudel sat alone in her apartment, waiting to be arrested. But no one appeared. The next afternoon, as she came out of a subway station, she was surrounded by police. The day had arrived.

Ida Nudel was charged with the crimes of "malicious hooliganism" and "slander against the state," which usually meant five years in a labor camp under a strict regimen. She was released to await trial on June 20. In the meantime, four KGB agents watched her constantly. To friends in the West, she wrote many letters and statements declaring that the charges were being used to punish her for her political activities. And to her family in Israel she wrote:

> Don't cry my dears, I think it is harder for you than for me because I am living the reality, even though it is a very difficult one, and you are forced to imagine what is happening to me.
>
> I emancipated my soul and I am at complete peace with my conscience. One has to pay for everything in this world; that is the law. Don't cry; without prison I will not gain freedom.

The trial of Ida Yakovlevna Nudel lasted only one day. She herself refused to participate because she knew the verdict was fixed from the start. It was supposed to be an open trial, but her friends were not allowed inside the courtroom. She wasn't even allowed to call her own witnesses.

Ida Nudel was sentenced to four years' exile in Siberia, the distant and vast region where Andrey Sakharov, Anatoly Sharansky, and Vladimir Slepak—like so many other political activists under the Soviet regime—lost years of their lives.

The Soviet government turned its back on the ideals of human rights and world peace by arresting Ida Nudel on the day the United Nations (pictured opposite) had designated for worldwide recognition of the rights of children.

Angel in Exile

Siberia—the dreaded place of exile—meant isolation, hard labor, and long, cruel winters. True, it was better than a prison sentence, but for Ida Nudel it turned out to be a daily struggle for food, warmth, and safety. She was sent to the tiny village of Krivosheino, on the River Ob, and left among suspicious strangers to find herself a job and a place to live.

For several months Nudel was the only woman in a factory dormitory, where she lived side by side with the crude men who were her co-workers. Finally, she found herself a log hut to live in and a new job as a night guard at a truck yard. Without a weapon for self-defense, she stood alone in the icy darkness. But she was grateful to have escaped the threats and insults of the men at the factory.

Still, survival in Siberia presented many other challenges. Despite her age, her small size, and a chronic heart ailment, Nudel walked a long distance every day in the bitter cold to get to and from her job. She had to haul buckets of water to her hut each day,

A snapshot taken by Ida Nudel of the village in Siberia where she lived for four years during her exile.

These Jewish immigrants from Tajikistan— a Muslim republic of the former Soviet Union— expresss their joy and relief as they finally arrive in Israel.

stoke the coal stove, raise chickens, and grow her own vegetables for sustenance. No one in the village would help since the KGB repeatedly warned the residents to stay away from her. No one seemed to care if she lived or died.

No one in Krivosheino, that is. But Ida Nudel's trial and exile had drawn worldwide attention to her situation and to the suffering of Soviet Jews in general. The letters of support were more numerous than ever, and so were the letters of protest sent to Soviet officials. Citizens of the world pleaded with their governments to intervene on her behalf. The knowledge that she was not forgotten carried her through the long, lonely years of exile.

Nor did Ida Nudel forget her Prisoners of Zion. She wrote to them even from Siberia. Anatoly Sharansky, who went to prison just a few months before Nudel's trial, recalls that she sent him letter after letter—more letters than anyone else except his mother and brother. Though only a few of her letters reached him, the prison officials made sure to let him know when mail from "that trouble-maker" had been confiscated. It was incredible to him that she was still doing so much for the prisoners. She even managed to send food and warm clothing to those who had less than she did.

Finally, in March 1982, Ida Nudel's sentence ended and she was allowed to leave Siberia. But the government was still not ready to let her go free. Not only was there no visa to Israel, but now there was no longer a permit for her to live in Moscow. Unable to return to her apartment, Nudel began another chapter of exile.

She had to find another place to live and obtain a residence permit from the local authorities, which was difficult for a former "criminal." She needed a place to live in order to be hired for a job, and she needed a job in order to get housing. Nudel wandered from city to city, feeling "like a homeless dog," until a Jewish family in Bendery, a town in the Moldavian Republic, invited her to live with them until she found work. Bendery was far from the activist Jewish community in Moscow, but at least it was not Siberia.

Mail continued to pour in, and the international campaign for Ida Nudel's freedom grew stronger. Among its participants were her sister, Ilana (Lena) Friedman; the U.S. secretary of state, George Shultz; and the actress and political activist Jane Fonda. Jane Fonda made many public appearances on Ida Nudel's behalf, and she urged members of the U.S. government to press for her release. She also telegraphed the highest authorities in Moscow and tried to get an audience with the Soviet ambassador in Washington.

When Jane Fonda announced that she would visit Ida Nudel in Bendery, the Soviet government could no longer ignore her. An international star calling on an enemy of the Soviet Union was bad enough, but refusing to allow Fonda to come would have been even worse. When the remarkable meeting of Jane Fonda and Ida Nudel finally took place, in November 1984, the visiting celebrity shook her head in amazement and exclaimed, "Such a great country is afraid of such a small woman!"

Freedom

Jane Fonda's visit provided a great boost to Nudel's spirits, but her situation still did not change. She wondered whether the Soviet leaders would ever tire of all the attention and see that it was really in their interest to let her go. She believed that she needed to get back to Moscow to keep up the pressure. Finally, early in the fall of 1986, Nudel was granted a hearing regarding her residence permit. She had been in Bendery for more than four years.

Nudel was already on her way to Moscow to plead her case when the police attempted to contact her in Bendery to tell her not to come. When she arrived at the apartment of her friends Leonid Bialy and Judith Ratner, a message was waiting for her.

"Sit down, Ida," Ratner said quietly, "I have something to tell you." Nudel was frightened by her friend's seriousness, then stunned by her words. "Ida," she said, "you have a visa."

Trembling with excitement, Nudel called the government visa office to find out whether the news was true. The chief himself got on the phone. "Yes, you have a visa," he said. "You must return to Moldavia immediately and they will explain everything to you."

Nudel was now convinced. Immediately, she placed a call to Lena in Israel, and the two sisters burst into tears of joy. Next she called Andrey Sakharov, the leading human rights activist in the Soviet Union, and several of her closest Moscow friends. Then the phone began to ring. One call after another came from reporters in the West, from supporters in Europe, America, and Israel. All over the world there was joy, relief, and renewed hope because Ida Nudel was finally free.

Nudel had waited fifteen years for a visa. Now she was given a deadline of October 20, less than three weeks, to prepare for her departure. On October 8, the head of the visa office called to say that she would be leaving even sooner. He told her that Armand Hammer, an American industrialist

Ida Nudel waited fifteen years for an exit visa. Now she lives on a moshav, an agricultural settlement, in central Israel.

with Moscow connections, would escort her to Israel on his private plane. Hammer believed that the go-ahead for Nudel's release had come directly from the general secretary of the Communist Party, Mikhail Gorbachev, who was interested in improving relations with the West. It was a clear turning point for the emigration movement.

One week later, on the evening of October 15, 1986, thousands of Israelis stood at Ben Gurion Airport on the lookout for the small plane with its special passenger. The excitement grew when the plane came into view, and when it touched down on the runway the crowd burst into applause. Finally the door opened and a small woman with gray hair and dark-framed eyeglasses emerged into the warm evening. Cheers arose, flags waved, and Hebrew songs of welcome filled the air as Ida Nudel descended the stairs. At the bottom she paused for a moment, smiled, and then stepped onto the ground of Israel.

Ida Nudel lives with her sister and brother-in-law on a moshav, *a rural settlement, in central Israel. She is the founder of Mother to Mother, an organization that provides support for single mothers who have emigrated from the former Soviet Union with their children. Ida Nudel is an active and vocal citizen of the Jewish state.*

CHAPTER 6

Shoshana S. Cardin
THE PRESIDENTS' PRESIDENT
(1926–   )

Shoshana Shoubin grew up in Baltimore, where the neighborhood Labor Zionist Center was the heart of her social life. She was always surrounded by people who cared passionately about the fate of the Jewish people. Her parents, Chana and Sraiah Shoubin, lived by the principle that all Jews are responsible for one another, and it was clear early on that their daughter also took that responsibility seriously.

As a child Shoshana raised money for the Jewish National Fund, gave political speeches, and was elected president of her Zionist youth group, Habonim. As an adult she made community service her career and eventually became the first woman to head the prestigious Conference of Presidents of Major American Jewish Organizations. In her weighty role as the official spokesperson for American Jewry, Shoshana Cardin has never been afraid to speak the truth—to say whatever has to be said—even when face-to-face with the most powerful leaders in the world.

*A*position of authority can be a lonely place. Shoshana Cardin first learned that lesson when she was still in her twenties, working in the Baltimore public school system. Cardin was hired as a substitute teacher for an eighth-grade English class composed mostly of fourteen- and fifteen-year-olds. Her students had already spent a year or two in the eighth grade and, they were proud to say, had already seen a parade of substitute teachers come and go. Now it was up to Cardin to take charge of this hostile bunch.

It didn't take long for her to size up the situation. Nelson, a hulking student who held the power in the class, was determined to see her fail. Each day he egged on the others with his wise-guy antics while Cardin tried to press ahead with her lessons. The showdown finally came when she announced to the class that she was going to be its permanent teacher.

"Oh no you're not. We'll get rid of you, too!" shouted a voice from the back of the classroom. Nelson sat there smirking, daring her to respond.

Shoshana Cardin knew this was a crucial moment. The class was waiting to see what she would do. There was no one to consult, no one to support her. She was on her own. With every appearance of calmness, she made her way down the aisle, stopped next to Nelson's desk, and glared down at him.

Nelson looked up. "For a nickel I would slap your face," he snorted, and Cardin knew the score: She had to meet his challenge on his terms, or she would lose the class. She returned to her desk, opened her purse, took out a nickel, and walked back to where Nelson sat.

"Put out your hand," she said firmly. She placed the nickel right on his palm, folded her arms, and waited.

Nelson held the nickel in his fingers for a moment. Then he stood up and threw it to the floor in disgust. Cardin had called his bluff. She had confronted the most powerful person in the room, asserted her authority, and earned the respect of all the students, even Nelson. Now, at last, she would be able to do her job.

Cardin completed the year with that eighth-grade class, but she did not return to teaching the following fall. In those days women were not allowed in the classroom if they were visibly pregnant, and between 1950 and 1957 she and her husband, Jerome Cardin, became the parents of four children. Shoshana Cardin chose to work instead as a community volunteer. She had the good fortune to be able to follow a calling for which the rewards are not monetary.

As the chairperson of the Conference of Presidents, Shoshana Cardin has talked face-to-face with many world leaders, including successive residents of the White House.

During 1991, Shoshana Cardin's new job as chairperson of the Conference of Presidents required quick, decisive responses to fast-breaking events, such as the war in the Persian Gulf (above) and (opposite) the breakup of the Soviet Union.

As Shoshana Cardin moved into positions of community leadership—first in her own city and state, then in major national organizations—the band of eighth-grade bullies became more remote. But the lessons she had learned in that classroom stayed with her. Never were they more valuable than in the fall of 1991, when Cardin was serving as chairperson of the Conference of Presidents of Major American Jewish Organizations. On two extraordinary occasions that fall, her responsibilities brought her face-to-face with the two most powerful leaders in the world: the president of the United States and the president of the Soviet Union.

"Where in the world did I get the courage to do those things?" Cardin asked herself later. And then she remembered that it began with Nelson.

The Right Message

Shoshana Cardin's tenure as chairperson of the Conference of Presidents began on January 1, 1991. She was the first woman ever elected to this central position in the Jewish community, but she had no trouble establishing her authority as the spokesperson for the forty-eight organization presidents who made up the conference. She herself was serving her third year as chairperson of the National Conference on Soviet Jewry, and she previously had been the first woman elected to head the Council of Jewish Federations. As a result, her name was already known and respected inside and outside the Jewish community and in the United States, Israel, and the Soviet Union.

People who have worked with Shoshana Cardin know her as an unusually serious, knowledgeable, and articulate person. They have also seen that even with all her talent and self-confidence, she has never shown interest in gaining power or recognition for herself. A traditional Jew, she is motivated by a deep commitment to the values of Judaism and a driving concern for the destiny of the Jewish people.

People have been ready to listen to Cardin because she is always thoughtful and well prepared. And because she takes a fair and open-minded approach to every issue, she has won the respect even of those who disagree with her. It was clear that Cardin could be counted on by members of the Conference of Presidents to represent a consensus of Jewish opinion and the best interests of the Jewish community.

For American Jews and Israelis, 1991 was a year of high tension. There was the war in the Persian Gulf, the crisis over U.S. loan guarantees to Israel, the stop-and-go movement toward a Middle East peace conference, the beginning of the breakup of the Soviet Union, and the rise of anti-Semitism in the Soviet republics.

The most controversial issue for American Jewry turned out to be Israel's request for a ten-billion-dollar credit endorsement, or

A demonstration near the Kremlin walls, Moscow, at the begining of the breakup of the Soviet Union.

loan guarantee, from the U.S. government. This guarantee would enable Israel to borrow huge sums of money from private banks and other institutions in order to build new housing for Russian immigrants. With the arrival of about 350,000 Soviet Jews in the late 1980s—pouring in at the average rate of about 10,000 a month — Israel's need for new housing was urgent.

The administration of President George Bush was unhappy that so much of Israel's new housing was planned for the West Bank and Gaza. The right to these areas, which had been occupied by Israel since the 1967 Six-Day War, was still a matter of dispute, and Bush believed it was impossible for Arabs and Israelis to talk about peace as long as the number of Jewish settlers in those territories was increasing. There would be no loan guarantee, he said, until Israel stopped building in the West Bank and Gaza.

All through the spring and summer of 1991, American Jews expressed the opinion that it was unfair to withhold the loan guarantee, which was so badly needly for the resettlement of Soviet Jews. But the Bush administration held firm. At the same time, however, a few members of Congress began to talk about taking legislative action to get the loan guarantee approved. A special task force of the Conference of Presidents decided to designate a day for concerned Jews to come to Washington, D.C., and speak about the matter with their representatives in Congress, urging them to act favorably when the question came to a vote.

President Bush was not at all pleased with this turn of events. He was annoyed with Congress for interfering with the president's role in making foreign policy decisions, and he was annoyed with the Jewish community for joining the effort to bypass his authority. Still the task force proceeded with its plans. The member organizations began to notify their individual members about the special mission to Washington, which was set for September 12. About 450 people signed up to participate.

On Friday, September 6, six days before the scheduled mission, Shoshana Cardin received a personal call from Lawrence Eagleburger, the deputy secretary of state. He told her that President Bush was still very unhappy about the whole affair, and he asked her to call off the "march on Washington" in the interest of avoiding an open confrontation.

"I'm sorry, I can't do it," Cardin replied firmly. She did not want a confrontation, but she could not give in on a matter that was so important to Israel.

"But why can't you?" the secretary pressed. "You know the president is going to have to speak out about what you're doing."

"I can't do it," she said, "because I would be sending the wrong message. It would be the wrong message to the Jews in the Soviet Union, to the Jews of Israel, and to the American Jewish community. It would say that we are not as serious as we really are."

"I'm willing to confront the president with that if I have to," Cardin concluded.

A Terrible Blow

What happened over the next five days was the opposite of what the Bush administration wanted. When the word spread that the president was "preparing for war" over the loan guarantees, the number of people signed up for the mission to Washington more than doubled. On September 12, approximately one thousand citizens arrived on Capitol Hill to call on their representatives in the House and Senate.

At noon on September 12, a very irritated George Bush called a news conference and put a surprising spin on the day's events. Portraying himself as under personal attack, he defended his view on the loan guarantees and his right to set foreign policy. He complained of the "powerful political forces" working against him and described himself as "a lonely little guy down here" with "something like a thousand lobbyists swarming all over the Capitol."

True, Shoshana Cardin had been warned by Deputy Secretary Eagleburger, but she never imagined that American Jews would hear their president say something so offensive and insulting. The president's remarks echoed the classic anti-Semitic slurs about a powerful Jewish lobby that controls the government and the press. In fact, the president's remarks touched off an outpouring of anti-Semitic phone calls and letters to the White House, congratulating the president for taking a tough stand and "speaking the truth" about the Jews.

The thousand Jews who visited Capitol Hill on September 12

These Jewish demonstrators in Washington, D.C. share Shoshana Cardin's belief that the right to petition government is a fundamental Constitutional right of every American citizen.

were not professional lobbyists, individuals who are paid by specific groups to represent their interests in Washington. They came to the Capitol that day as private citizens exercising a fundamental Constitutional right to petition their government. There was nothing unfair about it, as the president implied.

Shoshana Cardin knew that the president's challenge had to be met with an immediate response. She quickly called a news conference for later that day. Then she drafted a formal statement expressing her deep concern that the president appeared to be denying Jews one of the basic rights of all Americans. Later that afternoon Cardin distributed her statement to the press and answered their questions.

She had made her views clear, yet she still felt a need to respond to the president directly. After consulting a few other people, she decided that a personal letter would be the best way to state her position. It was a forthright letter in which she rejected the president's description of what had taken place on September 12. She tactfully suggested that his remarks had triggered negative responses that she was certain he had not wished to elicit. On September 13, she sent the letter to the White House, but she did not release it to the press or distribute it to the other members of the Conference of Presidents.

A week later, on the morning of September 21, Shoshana Cardin picked up her copy of *The New York Times* and read on the front page: BUSH ACTS TO CALM ISRAEL AID UPROAR. The article reported that President Bush had "sent a conciliatory letter . . . to reassure Jewish groups after his harsh attack last week. . . ." She eagerly turned to page 4 for the full text.

Cardin gasped. The letter was addressed to her—"Dear Shoshana"—and yet she had not seen it before. A few days earlier the White House had notified her that the president would soon reply to her letter of September 13, but there was no hint that the reply would be by way of a major newspaper.

Cardin was taken aback, but she had to be pleased. After all, her letter had drawn a public acknowledgment from the president of the United States. Nonetheless, she had a feeling that George Bush didn't fully understand the implications of what he had said and why it hurt the Jews so much. She made up her mind that at some moment in the future she would explain it to him again, preferably in a face-to-face encounter.

Confrontation at the Kremlin

Just a few weeks later Shoshana Cardin was on her way to Moscow, hoping for a face-to-face meeting with Soviet President Mikhail Gorbachev. During her presidency of the National Conference on Soviet Jewry (1988–1992), Shoshana Cardin visited the former Soviet Union several times a year, accompanied by Martin Wenick, the executive director of the organization. It was important for them to maintain direct contact with the Jewish communities and to meet frequently with Soviet officials about anti-Semitism and emigration.

In the fall of 1991, the number of Jews allowed to leave the Soviet Union was rising, but refuseniks were still being held on grounds of "secrecy," and no fair emigration law had yet been enacted. Jewish groups were also concerned about the activities of Pamyat, a vicious anti-Semitic group that was blaming the Jews for all of their country's misfortunes. Shoshana Cardin and Martin Wenick wanted to discuss these issues with President Mikhail Gorbachev. No official representative of American Jewry had ever had a personal meeting with a Soviet head of state, but Cardin and Wenick hoped for a change of heart at the Kremlin. After all, Gorbachev seemed to be more serious than ever about desiring openness and reform in his country.

When Cardin and Wenick arrived in Moscow on Monday, September 30, there was still no word about the requested meeting. Finally, at 10:00 P.M. on Tuesday evening, a phone call came to their hotel with the all-important message: Mr. Gorbachev would see them the next day.

Late Wednesday afternoon a taxi drove through the imposing gates of the Kremlin, the center of Soviet power, with Martin Wenick and Shoshana Cardin in the backseat. Even the Russian driver was nervous. A few minutes later the two visitors were led into a huge office, where President Gorbachev sat at his desk, talking on the telephone. In an instant he had replaced the receiver and was walking toward them with an outstretched hand and a welcoming smile. He escorted his guests to a table where, following the rules of diplomacy, the representative of American Jewry sat directly across from him. Wenick was at Cardin's side, and a Russian interpreter sat next to Gorbachev, who does not speak English.

It was an incredible moment. Shoshana Cardin thought of the pogroms in czarist Russia, the murders of Jewish doctors and writers under Joseph Stalin, the ordeal of the Prisoners of Zion, the ruthlessness of the KGB. Now she was face-to-face with the leader of this people who had caused so much Jewish suffering, and it was up to her to say what needed to be said.

She began by expressing the gratitude of American Jews for the recent increase in the number of Soviet Jews permitted to emigrate to Israel. She was concerned, however, about the number of refuseniks still being held for reasons of "secrecy." She urged Gorbachev to comply fully with international standards for freedom of emigration. Then she raised the subject of anti-Semitism and Pamyat. She said that American Jews were upset that the greater tolerance for freedom of expression in the Soviet Union seemed to be resulting in freer expression of anti-Semitism. She asked

Gorbachev to take a stronger stand against it. In fact, she had a specific request.

A few days later the American Jewish leaders would be attending a memorial ceremony at Babi Yar, the ravine near Kiev where nearly thirty-four thousand Jews were brutally murdered by the Nazis in 1941. That week was the fiftieth anniversary of the infamous massacre. It was a most appropriate time, Cardin suggested, for the first public statement from the Kremlin condemning anti-Semitism.

"I can't do that," Gorbachev replied. His response was polite but firm.

"May I ask why not?" Cardin said respectfully.

"There are many different nationalities in the Soviet Union," he explained. "To single out one of them would not be beneficial."

Then Gorbachev spoke of his own needs. He asked for Cardin and Wenick's help in obtaining American support for his reforms. He needed economic aid, and he hoped they would appeal to the

Even when talking with the most powerful people in the world, Shoshana Cardin has never been afraid to speak the truth. Here, she sits opposite Soviet President Mikhail Gorbachev in the Kremlin in the fall of 1991.

White House on his behalf. He was afraid that the Soviet Union
would disintegrate without it. The result, he believed, would be
economic chaos and even greater hostilities among the different
ethnic groups.

This observation brought Shoshana Cardin back to the subject
of anti-Semitism. At Babi Yar, she said, there would be messages
delivered from the president of the United States, the chairman of

*Shoshana Cardin
meets with U.S.
President Bush.*

the U.S. Holocaust Commission, and the president of the Ukraine.
Wouldn't it be fitting for the president of the Soviet Union to also
send a statement condemning anti-Semitism?

"Look, I cannot do this," he repeated. "But I do want you to
know that I understand what you are talking about because as a
child I saw Nazi atrocity for myself."

"But, Mr. President," she persisted, "there is a difference between what you say to us here privately and what should be said publicly, now and at Babi Yar."

Mikhail Gorbachev had no further comment. The meeting ended pleasantly, with Shoshana Cardin believing she had tried her best. At a press conference immediately afterward she announced that the Soviet president had promised to review the cases of 355 individuals who had been denied permission to emigrate. She said he acknowledged that anti-Semitism is a problem in the Soviet Union but did not believe it would be helpful to issue a statement condemning it at this time.

One hour later, over the radio, Cardin learned of Gorbachev's final decision on the matter. President Gorbachev, an announcer reported, had just issued a statement condemning anti-Semitism. His longtime aide, Aleksandr Yakovlev, was scheduled to be at Babi Yar for the commemorative ceremonies, and he would deliver that message on Gorbachev's behalf.

The following Monday morning a headline in *The New York Times* said it all: GORBACHEV CONDEMNS ANTI-SEMITISM, PAST AND PRESENT. It was the first such statement ever made by a Russian leader.

Alone with the President

Shoshana Cardin has always believed that a few individuals—even one individual—can have a significant impact on events, but she never dreamed she could have such an impact on the president of the Soviet Union. Perhaps that experience boosted her courage to speak the truth to the president of the United States as well. She still had that message she wanted to deliver to him personally on behalf of America's Jews.

A few weeks later she saw her opportunity. When the White House called to schedule a meeting with the Conference of Presidents in New York City on the afternoon of November 12, she decided to request a private visit with President Bush beforehand. She didn't say why, though the White House assumed it was about the loan guarantee. On November 9, Cardin received a reply: Yes, the president would see her.

Over the next three days Shoshana Cardin reviewed what she would say to George Bush. She consulted Malcolm Hoenlein, the executive vice chairman of the Conference of Presidents, who usually accompanied her in "private" meetings with government officials. She told him that she wanted to explain very plainly why the president's words had been such a terrible blow. Hoenlein agreed with her plan but warned her to be careful. By then it was understood that the loan guarantees would be granted. George Bush had done a lot for Israel, and he was, after all, the president of the United States.

At about 3:30 P.M. on November 12, Shoshana Cardin and Malcolm Hoenlein arrived at the Waldorf-Astoria Hotel in New York City, where the meetings were to be held. They rode the elevator to the twelfth floor and followed two Secret Service men along a circuitous route to the presidential suite. Bobbie Kilberg, the White House liaison for community affairs, stopped them at the door.

"I'm sorry," she said, "but Shoshana is going in alone."

"What?" Cardin was stunned. "But we talked about the two of us going in—it's always the two of us," she said.

"No, this time it's just you." Kilberg repeated. And Cardin was on her way to meet the president—alone.

The president, however, was not alone. With him were his national security adviser, Brent Scowcroft; his chief of staff, John Sununu; and his speechwriter, Richard Haas, who was responsible for the president's September 12 remarks. Bobbie Kilberg and two other presidential aides were also present. The president greeted Cardin warmly and motioned her to the sofa. It was an informal arrangement of people, with the president sitting on a straight-backed chair angled to face the entire group. After a few moments of introductions and greetings, Shoshana Cardin took a deep breath and went right to the point.

"Mr. President," she said, "I have a very important message for you, one that I never thought I would have to deliver to a president of the United States in this half century."

The president gave her his full attention. It was up to her to tell it to him straight.

"Mr. President," she continued, "it's about the statement you made on September 12. When you made those remarks about the Jews who descended on Washington that day, you tore the threads of the security net that we had woven around ourselves in thinking that we were full American citizens. When you tore that net, you drew blood, and the sharks came swimming."

Shoshana Cardin spoke quietly, but her words were powerful—so powerful that the president was appalled. His face was white. He stood up and turned his chair around to face her directly.

"But what did I say?"

"You gave the impression that we were powerful lobbyists, and when you did that, you invited anti-Semites to come forward and have their say."

"But I didn't specifically mention the Jews, did I?" the president countered.

"No, you didn't," Cardin said. "You didn't have to. It was very clear to us and to every-one. It was offensive," she went on, "and it was personally painful. It's the personal pain that I wanted to share with you, Mr. President, because I don't think you wanted to hurt anybody."

"I certainly did not," the presi-dent replied, and for several minutes he offered sincere words of apology. He was truly distressed by what he'd learned. "Shoshana," he said, "I would like you to open the meeting today and tell the others about this conversation. I would like you to convey my apology."

"Mr. President," she replied, "I beg to differ with you. I don't think I should open the meeting with this."

"No?"

"No, I think you should."

The president was uncomfortable. "I really would prefer that you do it, Shoshana."

"Mr. President," she said, "I think this is your responsibility."

And that is how the meeting opened—with a sincere apology from the president of the United States to the representatives of the American Jewish community.

A leader among leaders, Shoshana Cardin dines with the late Yitzhak Rabin, prime minister of Israel.

"Shoshana was very direct with me," George Bush said, "about the pain that I inadvertently caused—Shoshana was kind enough to say 'inadvertently.'" He was truly sorry, and he wanted them to know it and to carry that message to the community. It was a dramatic moment, one that none of the representatives had expected, and when the president finished speaking, everyone sat speechless.

Shoshana Cardin waited. With a room full of presidents of Jewish organizations, she thought that surely someone else would have something to add. But no one did. After all, their elected leader had once again spoken the truth to a person of power and had achieved something amazing. What more, then, could any one of them say?

On behalf of everyone present, Shoshana Cardin thanked the president for his understanding and for his apology to the Jewish community. Then she turned to the agenda before her and proceeded with the meeting. There was still a great deal of important business to address.

After her two-year term as chairperson of the Conference of Presidents, Shoshana Cardin became president of Clal, the National Jewish Center for Learning and Leadership. In 1994, she became the first woman to head the United Israel Appeal, an organization that plays a central role in raising and allocating money for the Jewish state.

CHAPTER 7

Nehama Leibowitz
TEACHER OF A NATION
(1905–)

*N*ehama Leibowitz was born into a well-to-do religious family in Riga, one of the centers of Russian Jewish culture. Her mother, Freydl, died while Nehama was still a child. Her father, Mordechai, was a strict parent who cared deeply about books, learning, and the education of his two children. Nehama and her older brother, Yeshayahu, were teenagers when their father brought them to Berlin, which was a great *center of intellectual life. There Nehama attended a German public school (gymnasium) and received the finest secular education available.*

At home Mordechai Leibowitz insisted on speaking Hebrew with his children, and he hired private tutors to instruct both his son and daughter in Jewish subjects. Nehama worked hard to keep up with Yeshayahu, and her father never hesitated to tell her that she was not meeting his expectations. But she persisted, and by the middle of the twentieth century the girl with the brilliant older brother had become the most influential teacher of Bible in the Jewish world.

"Nehama Leibowitz is the most outstanding living Israeli rabbi," a well-known Israeli scholar wrote in 1965. This may sound like an outrageous statement to make in a country where the ordination of women rabbis was, and remains, unacceptable to the religious establishment. To make such a statement about Nehama Leibowitz, a modest Orthodox woman who never imagined herself in the role of *rav*, a rabbinic authority, is all the more preposterous. But rabbi also means "teacher"—literally, "my teacher"—and in that sense the scholar, Rabbi Pinchas Peli, made a claim that is hard to dispute: In her role as teacher, no Israeli has done more than Nehama Leibowitz to bring the ethics and values of Torah into the lives of Jewish people.

That statement may sound like an exaggeration. After all, in Israel everyone studies the Bible. The Hebrew Bible, known as Tanakh, is a central text of the school curriculum, religious and nonreligious, from kindergarten through high school. In a society filled with students and teachers of Bible, how can one person have had such a singular impact?

But Nehama Leibowitz is unique, and everyone knows it. Some people call her a living institution. It would be hard to find an Israeli who hasn't read her newspaper column on the weekly Torah portion, heard her teach on the airways of the Israel Broadcasting

Service, consulted one of her many books, or seen her brown-clad figure ducking into a taxi as she rushes from one class to another. And it would be hard to find a teacher of Bible in the entire Jewish world who has not been influenced by her methods.

No Dry-as-Dust Thing

For anyone born in the last quarter of the twentieth century, especially in the United States, a world without female rabbis and female scholars of Judaica may be hard to imagine. Today women study Bible and Talmud in universities, in rabbinical schools of the Reform, Conservative, and Reconstructionist movements, and in Orthodox institutes for women's learning. But early in the twentieth century, when Nehama Leibowitz entered the world of serious Jewish study, it was a strange and unacceptable thing for a woman to do. Women were virtually excluded from the communal study of sacred texts, and it was considered foolish—even dangerous—for a man to teach his daughter Torah.

Ironically, it was Mordechai Leibowitz, Nehama's ever-critical father, who made sure his daughter had the opportunity to learn Torah, and he expected her to take it seriously. From her childhood years in Riga through her adolescence in Berlin, he provided private tutors for Nehama and her older brother, Yeshayahu. Even when the family went on summer vacations, a tutor came along, and the lessons in Jewish subjects did not cease.

Throughout her youth Nehama lived in the shadow of her brother, who became a brilliant scientist and philosopher. But she, too, was blessed with an extraordinary mind. As her intellectual talents grew, so did her pleasure in studying Torah. While a university student in Marburg, Germany, she began to give private lessons in Bible. As a graduate student she earned a doctoral degree for her work on Jewish-German translations of the Bible. It was an extraordinary achievement for any young woman at the time, and especially for a religious Jewish woman.

Germany was then an exciting place for a Jewish intellectual to be, but once Nehama earned her doctorate, she was ready to leave that world behind. Deeply affected by the ideals of religious Zionism, she longed to teach the texts she loved in the land where they made the most sense—*ki mi Tzion teitzei Torah* ("because from

Zion comes forth Torah"). After her marriage, to Lipman Leibowitz, an older man who was related to her father, Nehama Leibowitz and her husband left Germany to begin a new life in Palestine. But when they arrived in Jerusalem in 1930, Nehama was disappointed to find that the study of Bible—so exciting to her—was a dry and mechanical activity. The Bible was treated as a text to be learned by rote, not probed and analyzed. Centuries of commentaries written by the sages of the Diaspora—even those of the great Maimonides—were no longer regarded as useful, now that the Jewish people were returning to their own land.

None of this made sense to Nehama. There was so much to learn in the study of Torah, and the commentators had so much wisdom to offer. She believed that students needed exposure to the commentators to help them explore the underlying ideas and values of the text. She wanted her students to see how the great sages struggled to understand a word or a passage, just as every reader of the Bible has to struggle.

As a new teacher at the Mizrachi Women Teachers Seminary in Jerusalem, Nehama Leibowitz taught Bible the only way that made sense to her. She reinstated study of the commentators, making their thoughts a central part of her course. She also drew insights from the works of modern Jewish thinkers and modern Hebrew writers. She didn't care whether these thinkers and writers agreed with her religious point of view, which was devoutly Orthodox, as long as their insights contributed to the understanding of Torah. Sometimes she even introduced ideas from the literature and philosophy of non-Jewish writers. She was a great believer in a principle of Maimonides: "Accept the truth no matter where it comes from."

Many of her insights came straight from *amcha*—people who are not rabbis or scholars or writers but just ordinary Jews. She took special pleasure in quoting the wisdom of a taxi driver, a physician, or a shopkeeper; a soldier, a housewife, or a factory worker. Wherever Leibowitz went, she opened her mind to the people she met, and she learned from them.

To Nehama Leibowitz, teaching is always a process of give-and-take. She never just lectured to her students, though lecturing was the typical approach to conveying knowledge in the classroom. To her, the purpose of education is not to convey knowledge but to

*Opposite:
Many of the young
women Nehama
Leibowitz taught at
the Mizrachi
Womens' Teachers
Seminary in
Jerusalem were
Holocaust survivors
who impressed their
teacher with a love
of learning Torah
for its own sake.*

stimulate thinking—not to pass on information but to promote
understanding. "No one remembers the content of what you teach,"
she has told countless future educators, "so you have to show students
how to find knowledge for themselves."

She showed her students the way by asking questions—questions
that opened their minds to the deeper meaning of the text. Any
class she taught, whether small or large, was always the scene of a

lively dialogue. Often the commentators seemed to be there, too, asking questions and debating their views. The result was a thrilling sense of the timeless themes in Torah.

The key was not simply to ask questions but to find the right questions to ask. Nehama Leibowitz would never forget the frustration she felt as a child during the weekly Bible quizzes with her father. Every Shabbat, Mordechai Leibowitz would sit with his children, open the Bible at random, and come up with a question about the most obscure detail on the page. Nehama was always in the dark and routinely scolded for her ignorance. Though her own teaching method also requires close attention to detail, that's where the similarity ends. Her goal is not to stump students but to draw them out, to get them to think, talk, and argue about the text so that the ideas and values of Torah come alive and seem relevant.

To Nehama Leibowitz, the important question is not what is stated in the text but why it is stated, not what happens but why it happens: Why did Joseph tell his brothers about his dreams of having power over them? Why did Moses smash the tablets of the covenant? Why are two different words used to express the same idea? And why does the Ramban disagree with Rashi's interpretation? She emphasizes the value of comparing and contrasting the views of several commentators, so that her questions often begin with a familiar phrase: "What is the difference between . . . ?"

"It is no dry-as-dust thing for you," Moses told the Israelites before he died, charging them to keep the Torah as a living legacy for future generations. No teacher has done more than Nehama Leibowitz to prove that this is so. In 1957, when she was not even halfway through her career, she received the prestigious Israel Prize for Education in recognition of her unique achievements in bringing Torah to life for all kinds of Jews.

A World of Students

Nehama Leibowitz's passion for the Torah and the Jewish people has led her to a surprising variety of settings in her seven decades of teaching. She has taught all over Israel—at army bases, community centers, village schools, kibbutz dining halls, youth-group meetings, teachers' seminaries, religious institutions, and universities. Wherever people expressed the desire to study Torah, she was eager to learn with them. And wherever she went, they begged her to return.

From 1930 until 1955, her primary teaching job was at the Mizrachi Women Teachers Seminary, where she trained thousands of young Bible teachers for Israel's schools. In 1956, she joined the faculty of Bar-Ilan University, and in 1968 she became Professor of Education at Tel Aviv University. She received many invitations from universities abroad, including some of the finest in the world, but would never accept an offer to teach outside of Israel. Instead, students from other countries have come to her. From the early 1950s into the 1990s, thousands of individuals from all over the world—college students on a year-in-Israel program, rabbinical students of all denominations, master teachers, and future teachers—had the thrill of attending her classes.

One of her first groups of visiting students was from the Herziliya Academy in New York, a high school with a strong emphasis on modern Hebrew. The class of seniors arrived in Israel in the fall of 1952 for a year of study at the Mizrachi Seminary. Expecting great things, they were surprised to learn that their Bible teacher would be someone named Nehama Leibowitz. Not only was she unknown to them, but their previous experience in serious Judaic study had always been with male instructors.

On the first day of class, this mystery woman handed out a sheet of questions about the Torah portion to be studied. They were her typical "why" questions, requiring precise analytic thinking about the text. She asked her bright young students to work through as many questions as they could. Then she collected their papers, read out their answers, and as one student recalls, "She put us in our place. We just didn't get what she was after." It dawned on them just how much they had to learn from her.

Each day the students' amazement and admiration grew. After a few months the group that had expected so little from a female teacher asked for more time in which to study with her. To them she became the ideal of the learned woman. They sensed her reverence for the Torah and marveled at her openness to hard questions and new ideas. These aspiring teachers were also amazed that she could teach students at so many different levels, from ten-year-old schoolchildren to university doctoral candidates.

Nehama Leibowitz was always a demanding teacher, intimidating to many. She didn't hide her annoyance with students who were not prepared for class, had forgotten a book, or could not read the Hebrew text with ease. One student whose reading of Hebrew was shaky recalls being sent from the class with another student who was in the same boat. Leibowitz instructed them not to return until they had read the entire Hebrew text to each other out loud. When they were finished, she graciously welcomed them back to the classroom.

Sooner or later most of her students also saw the warm and caring side of their teacher. To the surprise of many, she seemed to enjoy encountering them outside the classroom and seized the opportunity for a personal chat. Many found that they could come to her for advice on serious personal issues. Even years later she remembered things about them and would recognize their faces—perhaps because she always focused on them so intently in the classroom.

Enrollment Unlimited

Over the years Nehama Leibowitz also developed special relationships with thousands of students whose faces she never saw at all. Countless individuals tuned in to the Israel Broadcasting Service each week for her popular lesson on the Torah portion. Many wrote to her with their own questions and comments, and every letter received a personal answer. But the vast majority of her "faceless" students were those who subscribed to her famous *gilyonot*, the study sheets she produced weekly for a vast network of students throughout the world.

The idea for the *gilyonot* grew out of a class that Leibowitz conducted for a small group of religious kibbutz women in 1941. The women had come to Jerusalem for six months of study and were so enthralled by their course with her that they begged for a way to continue it. Always ready to nurture an interest in Torah, she offered to teach them by mail—that is, to prepare a study sheet for each week's Torah portion. Each sheet would include selected commentaries to analyze and questions to answer.

Every week for a year Leibowitz mailed mimeographed study sheets to the women in their respective kibbutzim. At the bottom of each sheet was the simple instruction: "Send your answers to Nehama Leibowitz, Kiryat Moshe, Jerusalem." When the answers came back to her, she read them carefully, marked them with her red pen, and returned them to the students.

The system worked. It worked so well that word spread, and others wanted to become Leibowitz's students-by-mail. The second year fifty students joined the "class"; the third year, three hundred; and soon the number was in the thousands.

By the late 1940s Nehama Leibowitz was conducting a one-person correspondence course on Torah with seemingly unlimited enrollment. Students mailed back *gilyonot* from all over Israel and from as far away as England, Morocco, the United States, and South Africa. Each year brought more requests for the study sheets, and each year Leibowitz prepared a new cycle of questions on the weekly Torah portion. What's more, she always included at least two levels of questions, the more difficult ones marked with asterisks so that more advanced students would be adequately challenged.

How one person handled this volume of work is almost impossible to imagine. And Nehama Leibowitz did it without the benefit of computers, fax machines, or E-mail. Finally, in 1960, she agreed to have the Torah Education and Culture Department of the Jewish Agency fill requests for the *gilyonot*, but she still insisted on checking the answers herself. For a time she tried to keep track of the number of sheets that she corrected. She stopped counting at forty thousand.

How did she do it? The explanation is beyond logic. What kept her going, says one close friend, is love—love for Torah and love for

Between her teaching and her published works, including her gilyonot, Nehama Leibowitz has transformed the study of Bible into a lively and relevant experience that is accessible to everyone who wants to learn.

Am Yisrael, the people of Israel. To bring the two together has always been the driving purpose in her life.

For the Joy of Torah

With such a huge volume of correspondence, Nehama Leibowitz could hardly get to know her "faceless" students individually. But over the years she was thrilled and amazed by the great variety of Jews who subscribed to the *gilyonot*. They were factory workers and kibbutz farmers; soldiers and members of parliament; doctors and professors; housewives and nurses; teenagers and senior citizens. One waitress wrote that she worked on the questions during her morning coffee break; a midwife, between deliveries at the hospital; a machinist, during lunch breaks at the factory; a soldier, in his tent near the battlefield. Was there anything, she wondered, that could keep these Jews from learning Torah?

Nehama Leibowitz was awed by the devotion of her students, and the feeling was mutual. All over Israel she was known affectionately and respectfully as *moratenu,* "our teacher." Always uncomfortable with lofty academic titles like Doctor and Professor, to be known simply as *mora* (teacher) was the recognition she valued most.

Nehama Leibowitz continued the *gilyonot* for thirty years, until the fall of 1971, when she announced the conclusion of her last series. Thirty years of study sheets—1,560 in all—would still be available through the Jewish Agency's Torah Department, but no new ones would be issued. The end of an era had come, and Leibowitz marked the transition with a farewell letter to her students. In closing she wrote:

I am enthralled by this vast army of old and young, mothers and girls, teachers male and female, clerks and laborers, veterans and newcomers of all communities, hundreds of thousands (literally) studying Torah for its own sake. For our joint studies involved no certificates, examinations, marks, prizes, or credits. . . . simply the joy so deep of the one who studies Torah.

It was Leibowitz who had brought that joy into their lives. Nehama Leibowitz was sixty-six years old when she concluded

the *gilyonot,* but retirement held no interest for her. With the death of her husband after many years of illness, and with no children or grandchildren to claim her time, she immersed herself in her work. When she was not teaching a class or traveling between classes, she could be found in her usual spot at the Jewish National Library in Jerusalem, surrounded by her beloved texts and commentators.

She was now devoting much more time to writing. One endeavor was a column called *Studies in the Weekly Sidra,* which appeared for seven years in Jewish newspapers throughout the Diaspora. She derived pleasure from knowing that many study groups were organized around her weekly articles and many rabbis were consulting them as they prepared their sermons.

She was also working hard to organize her Torah studies for publication. The result is a series of volumes covering each of the five books of Moses. These books, published by Israel's Ministry of Education and Culture, have been translated into English, French, Spanish, and Dutch. They are used in homes, libraries, and synagogues throughout the world.

The Rabbi's Rebbe

It is difficult to imagine what the study of Bible would be like today without the contributions of Nehama Leibowitz—her radio broadcasts, her *gilyonot,* her columns, her books, and her thousands of disciples. She has transformed the study of Bible into a lively and relevant experience that is accessible to everyone who wants to learn.

For Jewish women in particular, Nehama Leibowitz has been a trailblazer, and in a way she never anticipated or even desired. She was not out to start a revolution in women's roles, only to follow her true calling as a Jew. Nevertheless, in her ceaseless efforts to understand the deeper meanings of Torah and to share them with other Jews, she set the precedent for Jewish women as serious students and teachers of Judaism.

Nehama Leibowitz has never joined in the public debate about ordaining women as rabbis, or about any other aspect of the role of women in Judaism. She does not think of herself as a pioneer or a role model. In fact, she doesn't like to draw attention to herself at all. She rarely gives interviews and prefers not to be written about. Whatever there is to know about her, she says, is in her books about Torah. That's where the attention belongs.

In 1987, however, after staying clear of publicity and controversy for so many decades, Leibowitz found herself at the center of a dispute over her right to do what she had been doing for more than half a century: teach Torah to all kinds of Jews. The controversy arose when the head of the Or Torah yeshiva, Rabbi Shlomo Riskin, invited Leibowitz to teach in one of his programs, an institute for training graduates of Israeli yeshivas to serve as rabbis throughout the Diaspora. One important part of the program would be the study of Chumash, the Five Books of Moses, since the sermons given by a congregational rabbi usually follow the cycle of weekly Torah readings.

Riskin knew from experience that Chumash is not taught in a serious academic way in the yeshiva world. When he came to Israel in 1960 as a rabbinical student from Yeshiva University in New York, Nehama Leibowitz had introduced him to an exciting new approach to Bible. Now he wanted the rabbis in his institute to have that experience, too. Naturally, Leibowitz accepted the invitation. She would gladly do what she had always done—namely, teach Torah to whoever wanted to learn with her.

But some members of Israel's rabbinic establishment were not happy with this arrangement. Rabbi Eliezer Schach, leader of the ultra-Orthodox Agudat Yisrael movement, said it was not proper for a woman to stand before a group of men engaged in the study of Torah. If Leibowitz continued to teach, Schach stated, he would place a ban on the program, meaning that former students of Agudah yeshivas would have to withdraw from the program.

Leibowitz was surprised by the fuss. For more than half a century she had taught both men and women with hardly a thought about their gender. But she did not protest or issue any public statement. As usual, she was not interested in causing a stir. And she did not want her former student, Rabbi Shlomo Riskin, to be in a difficult situation because of her. Privately, she offered to resign.

But Riskin did not yield to the pressure. He did not yield to the threat that half the participants in the program would leave if their rebbe imposed the ban. For a quarter century Nehama Leibowitz had been Shlomo Riskin's "rebbe" for Chumash, and as long as she was willing to teach in his program, he felt fortunate to have her there. "I want to give these rabbis the best that Israel has to offer," he told reporters, "and there's no question about it—Nehama Leibowitz is Israel's best."

Leibowitz continued to teach at the Or Torah institute. Half the students and teachers honored the ban and withdrew from the program. The following year enrollment was higher than ever.

Nehama Leibowitz was in her late eighties when she decided to stop rushing from place to place and to conduct classes only in her home. There, in her two-room apartment behind the Jerusalem bus station, surrounded by shelves packed with books and crammed with gilyonot, she continues to meet with small groups of students almost every day of the week. It is something of a miracle, her students say, to see her frail body become infused with energy and her worn face turn radiant each time she immerses herself in the joy and wisdom of Torah.

CHAPTER 8

Yael Arad

OLYMPIC CHAMPION
(1967–)

In the summer of 1972, the eyes of Israel turned to Munich, where the world's best athletes were gathering for the Summer Olympic Games. Yael Arad hardly noticed. Born in Israel in 1967, she was too young to understand what it meant for Israel to send a team of athletes to Germany, the country that had tried to wipe out the Jewish people during World War II. But she was aware of the outpouring of grief all around her when eleven members of Israel's Olympic team were murdered there by Palestinian terrorists.

Twenty years after that tragic event, Yael Arad had Munich on her mind when she became a member of Israel's delegation to another Summer Olympiad, this one in Barcelona, Spain. In Barcelona she accomplished what no Israeli, man or woman, had ever done before, and she reminded the world of the eleven martyred athletes who never had their chance to try.

*B*arcelona, July 26, 1992: It was a week into the Olympic Games when Yael Arad, Israel's best hope ever for an Olympic medal, arrived on the scene. For the past two years she had woken up each morning to train for Barcelona, the pressure building as the months passed. All she had to do now was get through the next three days—settle in, warm up, try to relax. Just three more days until July 30, when the twenty-five-year-old Israeli would go for the gold.

Yael Arad was one of the top three female judoka in the world. She had already won a bronze medal at the 1991 World Championship in Barcelona and a gold medal at the 1992 French Open in Paris. Now she was back in Barcelona, determined to prove herself a champion in the first-ever Olympic competition for women's judo.

Arad had a few other things to prove as well. Touted everywhere as Israel's ticket to Olympic glory, she was out to put an end to her country's long dry years of waiting. For forty years Israel had been sending athletes to the Olympic Games, but there wasn't a single medal to show for it. What was holding the Israeli athletes back, Arad believed, was a "mental barrier" about achievement in sports. Because no Israeli had ever won at the Olympics, Israelis didn't believe they could. Yael Arad was out to change all that.

"It's so much harder when you have no tradition of winning," she explains. "When no one before you has done it, it's much harder to believe that you can. In Israel the tradition used to be that you'd go to the Olympic Games and people wouldn't even expect you to succeed." Without the moral support that athletes need, and without the financial backing that many other countries provide for their Olympic hopefuls, many talented Israeli athletes just give up altogether.

And then there is the Munich massacre, which has surely discouraged a more positive Israeli attitude toward Olympic competition. As eager as she was to compete at Barcelona, Yael Arad often found herself thinking about those Israelis who went to Munich to perform their best as athletes and came back dead because they were Jews. Ever since Munich the security for Israel's Olympic team had been very tight, but Arad and her family still had safety on their minds.

Stronger than the anxiety, though, was her desire to give the Olympic world a new image of Israel's athletes. Instead of seeing coffins being carried from the Olympic Village, she wanted the world to see an Israeli athlete standing proudly on the medalists' platform under her country's blue-and-white flag. The message would be clear: "Look, everybody. The terrorists did not stop us. We're still here, and we're strong, and we're winners."

It was a lot to think about: avenging the murder of eleven Israeli sportsmen, giving Israel the Olympic victory it had never had, providing Israelis with a new self-image regarding sports, and winning the gold medal she had worked so hard for. But wasn't it time for it all to come together?

Mind Versus Muscle

Yael Arad's journey to the Olympic Games had begun sixteen years earlier, the first time she visited the Maccabee Tel Aviv sports club, where her three older brothers learned judo. As a child Yael took to every sport she tried but she knew right away that judo was special. Of course, she wasn't thinking about going to the Olympics at that point, just that she loved the sport and wanted it to be hers.

At that time, in the late 1970s, judo was not a popular sport in Israel. At Maccabee Tel Aviv there were only seven other children in her age group practicing judo, and all of them were boys. In fact, throughout her childhood only two other girls were among her judo companions. But that never bothered Yael. "It was such a great feeling," she remembers, "to stand in front of another child my same size—usually a boy—and know that I could throw him!"

In judo, "throwing" your opponent is one of the specific moves that can be used to win a match. Each move that is successfully performed is awarded a certain number of points, and the highest scorer after four minutes is the winner. A tie is settled by a decision of the judges. A judo competition, like a tennis tournament, is composed of a series of matches. The champion is the one who wins four or five consecutive matches in total.

Winning at judo is not just a matter of physical power, as in boxing or wrestling. What makes judo special is that the fighter must figure out how to use his or her opponent's power as well. Yael Arad explains: "If you push me, I don't push you back, I pull you; I use your power to perform my move." It's an approach that can apply to many areas of life, which is why judoka often react calmly to whatever comes their way. The practice of judo helps them develop self-confidence and self-control.

"What I love about judo," Arad says, "is that it requires a combination of physical power and mental power. You have to think in order to win. You have to be stronger, smarter, and faster than your opponent." Arad also loves the artistry of the sport, with its ceremonial white uniforms and precision of movement. She sees judo as an art in which she can express herself as an individual through nuances of movement and technique.

It was clear from the start that Yael Arad was a natural at putting all the elements of judo together—the strength, the concentration, and the artistry. By the time she was ten years old, she was Israel's junior champion, the best judoka in the under-fourteen category. Her coach declared that she was born to be a champion.

Yael's success at judo took her parents by surprise. Both are journalists, and they had never imagined that their daughter would become an athlete. But they wanted Yael to pursue her interests and explore her talents, so they gave her the support she needed—uniforms, lessons, rides back and forth to the judo club, and most important, constant encouragement.

When Yael was nearly sixteen, her parents permitted her to

Oppostite: Winning a medal at the Olympic Games represents the pinnacle of athletic achievement and brings great honor to the medal-winner's native country.

*Determination,
self-discipline, and
a great love for the
sport have sustained
Yael Arad through
years of training
and competition.*

travel abroad with her judo club to take part in international competitions. Exploring the world outside Israel was exciting in itself. But competing with young people from other countries, especially countries that were accustomed to turning out champion athletes, was a big step for Yael psychologically. The foreign athletes seemed to her to have the clear advantage, while she felt herself competing against the odds.

Yael eventually realized that her main obstacle was the Israeli mental barrier to achievement in sports. She broke through it when she understood that each of her competitors, no matter what coun-

try she comes from, is only another human being. If any of them can become a world champion, she told herself, then so can I.

Yael looked around her and saw many young women with talent in judo, but she also understood that becoming a champion takes much more than talent. Only a few will become champions, she told herself, and it's the hard work and discipline that will make the difference. She knew that if she were willing to expend the effort, she, too, could reach a top rank in her sport.

People often ask Yael Arad what she had to give up in order to become a judo champion, but she does not see her success in terms of sacrifice. "You could say that I have given things up," she smiles, "but the truth is that I gave them up in order to gain other things. I've had so many things that most people my age never have, like traveling abroad so often, seeing different cultures, meeting different people, and of course the satisfaction of achieving my personal goal.

"It feels good to know that everything you're doing is for one purpose. But you have to decide: Are you willing to give everything you have to your goal or not? Not many people can do it because they can't see the distant future and know what will be in ten or fifteen years. . . . You just have to believe in yourself."

With the wholehearted support of her family and the expert guidance of her coaches, Yael worked hard to keep raising her level of performance. By August 1990, she was ranked seventh in Europe in women's judo. Along the way she also finished high school, completed her military service, and began to study nutrition at the Weizmann Institute of Science in Israel. But with the next Olympic Games barely two years off, Yael realized she would have to train even harder to have a shot at a medal. Was it possible? Was she willing to put everything else on hold in order to reach that next level of achievement?

On to Barcelona

Yael Arad's fighting spirit prevailed. She postponed her college studies and committed herself to full-time training for the Barcelona Olympics.

Arad's new training program, developed by her longtime judo coach, Danny Leopold, consisted of fourteen sessions a week—

about seven hours a day. Five times a week she attended the regular
training sessions of the women's judo team. For her other nine sessions she followed an individualized program, which combined judo
practice with various types of strength training and aerobic exercise.
Arad and Leopold also spent time analyzing videotapes of judo
matches, her own and her prospective opponents'. She worked with
a fitness coach to improve her overall conditioning and with a
sports psychologist to strengthen her self-confidence.

For strength training, Arad did push-ups, sit-ups, and free-
weight exercises, thus working all the different muscle groups in her
body. For aerobic exercise, she went for bicycle rides, took long jogs
on the beach, and took part in other seasonal sports. When it came
to her intensive judo training, she sparred with Shai Yona and Amit
Lang of the national men's team; no other woman on Israel's team
could provide Arad with enough of a challenge.

The strict training regimen paid off. Back in 1989, Arad had
promised herself that she would build up to the Olympics by winning a medal in every competition she entered over the next two
years. And she kept that promise. During 1990 and 1991, she won
bronze medals at judo competitions held in Finland, Holland, and
Germany and silver medals at the competitions in France,
Scandinavia, and Great Britain. Her first major international
achievement was winning the bronze medal at the 1991 World
Championship in Barcelona. Then came the real breakthrough, in
February 1992, when she took the gold medal at the prestigious
French Open in Paris. For the first time in international competition, Arad heard the band play "Hatikvah," Israel's national
anthem. Her dream of hearing it played at the Summer Olympics
was now a huge step closer to reality.

After placing third in the 1991 World Championship at
Barcelona, Yael Arad was an instant hero in Israel. The media were
obsessed with her prospects for an Olympic gold medal, and Israelis
suddenly took her achievements seriously. She even acquired a few
sponsors, including the Israeli newspaper La'Ishah ("for the woman"),
who supplemented the small amount of money she was receiving
from the Israel Sports Federation.

With the Israeli public so focused on Arad's chances of bringing
home a medal, no one seemed to appreciate—or even notice—how

much she had already done for her country simply by being out there in the international field. As a world-class athlete, Arad found that she was representing Israel in many ways. She discovered that she could be a kind of ambassador-at-large for a country that was often misunderstood in many parts of the world.

When Arad traveled to international competitions in Europe or to judo training camps in Japan, she often met athletes who knew almost nothing about life in Israel. Many had never before met anyone from her country. They knew only what they saw on television: gunfire, bombings, stonings, ambushes, and the like. To the world outside, Israelis were either soldiers with rifles or bearded men in black hats. But Yael Arad, a personable, soft-spoken young woman—an athlete like them—presented a different picture of what Israel is all about. People asked questions about life in the Jewish state, and Arad was glad to provide the kind of answers that can come only from someone born and raised there. They talked about everything from wars and politics to popular music and lifestyles, and of course they talked about their common experiences as athletes.

One subject that other athletes never asked her about was the massacre at the Munich Olympics. Nor did Arad raise it, though the massacre is a significant part of her own identity as an Israeli athlete. Each year Israelis would pause for a memorial to the eleven martyrs, but the rest of the sports world seemed to have forgotten them. Since 1972, there had not even been a moment of silence for them at any of the Olympic Games.

With the approach of the 1992 Summer Olympics, Arad found herself thinking more about Munich. She was out of the country when the memorial ceremony took place that spring, and she felt she had missed something important. She needed to do something as an act of remembrance before she left for Barcelona. After discussing her feelings with her brother Yuval, she decided that she would try to meet with some of the families of the murdered athletes.

Soon she had arranged to visit with Anki Spitzer, widow of the fencing coach Andrey Spitzer, and Elana Romano, widow of the weight lifter Yosef Romano. They would all meet at the home that Anki Spitzer had made with her new husband and their children. Anki's daughter Anna, who was four months old when her father

The Israeli Olympic team proudly displays the Israeli flag at the opening ceremony of the Munich Olympics in 1972. Just days later, Arab terrorists murdered eleven Israeli athletes and their coaches in the Olympic Village.

was killed, would join them as well.

The meeting took place early in July, and it turned out to be a happy experience for all who took part. Arad's visit let the families of the murdered athletes know that the new generation of Israeli athletes had not forgotten what they endured. Their warmth and enthusiasm told her that they would be with her in Barcelona. She felt their interest in her career, their excitement about her Olympic debut, and their prayers for her success. Before the visit ended, Anki Spitzer's husband gave Arad a small volume of the Psalms, which are traditionally recited at the outset of a trip to ask God's blessing along the way. Yael Arad is not a religious Jew, but the gift moved her deeply. It has a permanent place in the bag she carries with her wherever she travels.

Silver or Gold?

Arad felt strengthened by her visit with Anki Spitzer and Elana Romano, but by the time she got to Barcelona the media—especially the Israeli media—were wearing her out. "I put a lot of

pressure on myself," she says, "and I don't need outside pressure in order to succeed." Always nervous before a competition, Arad knows that she has to turn that nervous energy into fighting energy. On July 30 in Barcelona, she succeeded in doing just that.

It was a long, complicated, and wondrous day. At 8:00 A.M. she weighed in, verifying her place in the under-sixty-one-kilogram category. Later in the morning she had a brief warm-up session. Mostly she waited, nervously. She made sure she was surrounded by people who understand what she's like when she's under that kind of pressure, and the pressure that day was greater than any she had ever felt before. Finally, at 1:00 P.M., she stepped onto the mat for her first round in the long-awaited competition.

Arad's first opponent was Begoña Gómez of Spain, who had beaten her twice in previous competitions. Gómez was of course the hometown favorite, and the arena was packed with Spaniards—6,000 screaming fans and only 250 of them Israelis. But Arad knows how to use a crowd, even if it is not cheering for her. "If the crowd is against me," she says, "I just say to myself, 'They want me to lose—Okay, I'll show them.'"

Arad expected a tough match. She also knew—from experience and from studying the videotapes of her opponent—exactly what she had to do in order to win. "My advantage," Arad says, "was that Gómez thought she had the advantage."

Arad was the winner and she moved on to her next match, this time against Marika Januchkova of Czechoslovakia. Arad had beaten Januchkova in the final round of the 1992 French Open, when she won her first gold medal. She went into her second match with confidence and came out with an easy victory.

The third match was against Germany's Frauke Eickhoff, a former world champion. Arad says it was probably the toughest match of her life, not only because Eickhoff was a formidable opponent but because the outcome had double significance. This was the semifinal

One of the terrorists looks out from the apartment where Israeli athletes are kept hostage.

round of the competition, and the winner would be assured at least a silver medal, plus a chance to compete for the gold in the final round. A silver medal would satisfy Israel's need for Olympic recognition. But Arad would be satisfied only with the gold.

Arad struggled against Eickhoff and after one minute she was down by three points. Then she hurled her opponent over in a swooping move that earned her an *ippon*, a full ten points. Eickhoff claimed the *ippon* was hers, not Arad's. But the judges had no question about whose it was. Arad was still holding Eickhoff down when she heard the judges' call in her favor. With a screech of pure joy, she leaped into the air and tumbled off the judo mat into the arms of Israeli team officials. At last she—and Israel—had their long-awaited Olympic medal.

But the day wasn't over. Still to come, two hours later, was the fourth and final round of the competition, in which Arad would compete against Catherine

Pictured opposite, Israeli fans cheer their first Olympic medal-winner when Yael Arad battles Germany's Frauke Eickhoff and France's Catherine Fleury (above).

Fleury of France. One of them would win the silver medal; the other would win the gold. Arad had defeated Fleury in the semifinal round of the French Open, but she knew that this one would not be an easy match. In fact, it was fierce and agonizing. The two women pushed and pulled and tumbled and held each other down, and in the end neither of them had earned any points. It was up to the judges to determine which woman had given the better performance. But the judges' vote was split, and it fell to the referee to break the tie. The referee pointed to Fleury.

Closing the Circle

Yael Arad proudly wears her Olympic silver medal. Twenty years after Munich, Yael Arad proved that Israeli athletes could compete and succeed in the international sports arena.

Fifteen minutes later Yael Arad stood under the flag of Israel on the platform of Barcelona's Olympic Stadium and received a silver medal. She had wanted so badly to hear "Hatikvah" played at the Olympics. Now, as the band played the French national anthem for Catherine Fleury, tears streamed down Arad's face.

"It was so emotional," she explains. "I lost, and I didn't want to lose, but after all, it was the first medal for Israel, and I was very excited about that."

Standing on the podium during the medal ceremony, overcome by so many conflicting emotions, Arad thought of the Munich martyrs. She decided right then that she would cap Israel's victory by doing something especially for them.

In a press conference after the ceremony, her silver medal shining on her chest, Arad broke the silence. She told the world that this was the right moment to remember the eleven Israeli athletes and coaches who had been killed twenty years earlier at the Summer Games in Munich. She announced that she was dedicating Israel's first Olympic medal to the victims and their families: "Maybe now we can say, if it is possible, that we have avenged this murder. I think we owe it to the families and to the people of Israel. . . . We'll never forget what happened, but maybe today is something that will close the circle."

In twenty years no one at the Olympics had made public mention of the massacre. Now everyone was talking about it. Reporters swarmed around Arad and bombarded her with questions. The next day Israel and the Munich massacre were in the headlines all over the world—only this time with the fresh new twist that Yael Arad had made possible.

Montreal: ISRAEL'S FIRST MEDAL RECALLS '72 MASSACRE

New York: TWENTY YEARS AFTER THE MASSACRE, ISRAEL REJOICES OVER A MEDAL

Washington, D.C.: ISRAEL CELEBRATES GREATEST OLYMPIC TRIUMPHS BY REMEMBERING TRAGEDY

Philadelphia: MEDAL HELPS DRY TWENTY YEARS OF TEARS

Los Angeles: TIME FOR ISRAEL TO ENJOY THE GAMES

Jerusalem: ARAD'S OLYMPIC MEDAL TAKES ISRAEL BY STORM

Back home in Israel it was a time for celebration. People danced in the streets of Tel Aviv. Fireworks exploded in the towns and villages. "The whole country is upside down with joy," said Shmuel Lalkin, director of the Israel Sports Federation. "Winning Olympic medals is a regular routine in America," he told a reporter from *The Washington Post*, "but in Israel it's a revolution."

It didn't matter that Yael Arad hadn't won the gold medal, though everyone agreed that she deserved it. She had done something wonderful for Israel, something more than anyone expected. As *The Jerusalem Post* said in its editorial:

> Yael Arad's modesty, her consciousness of the legacy of the massacre of the Israeli sportsmen at Munich twenty years ago and her visits to the victims' families on the eve of her departure for Barcelona make her more than just a talented sportswoman. She is a person of whom the nation can justly be proud.

The Barcelona Olympics had barely come to a close when people began to ask Yael Arad about competing in Atlanta in 1996. Regardless of her decision, she had already made a lasting impact on what would happen there. Because of Yael Arad, Israel's athletes can go to Atlanta, and to all future Olympic Games, with the knowledge and confidence that they, too, are strong enough to be winners.

Acknowledgments

I am indebted to many authors who have previously written about the women in this book and to many individuals who were willing to share their knowledge and experience in personal interviews with me.

Of the eight women who are the primary subjects of these chapters, Henrietta Szold is the one whose life is best documented. My understanding of her was enhanced by the work of several biographers: Irving Fineman, Elma Ehrlich Levinger, Marvin Lowenthal, Rose Zeitlin, and especially Joan Dash. Dash's book, *Summoned to Jerusalem* (New York: Harper & Row, 1979) is the most recent and comprehensive treatment of Szold's life. However, despite the important role that Szold played in the rebuilding of Palestine, she receives little prominence in most Zionist histories.

Of the many books about the Holocaust, and about the Warsaw Ghetto in particular, only a few describe the important role that Zivia Lubetkin played. I have drawn primarily on her own memoir, *In the Days of Destruction and Revolt* (Tel Aviv: Hakibutz Hameuchad, 1981) and on Yitzhak Zuckerman's *A Surplus of Memory* (Berkeley: University of Calif., 1993), for details about the uprising that both of them helped to lead.

Rose Schneiderman's role in the Jewish labor movement is noted in many general works of Jewish history and labor history. A full account of her activities during the early years of the labor movement is found in her autobiography, *All for One* (New York: P.S. Eriksson, 1967). Lillian Wald writes about Rose Schneiderman in *The House on Henry Street* (New York: H. Holt & Co., 1915), her memoir of life on the Lower East Side. For information on the Triangle Fire in particular, I relied on extensive coverage of the event in *The New York Times* and on Leon Stein's comprehensive volume, *The Triangle Fire* (Philadelphia: Lippincott, 1962).

Ida Kaminska's autobiography, *My Life, My Theater* (New York: Macmillan, 1973), was my best source of information about the off-stage life of this great actress. Of the many articles written about Ida Kaminska and her theater, two that appeared in the journal *Midstream* were especially helpful: "Ida Kaminska in Exile," by Mendel Kohnsky (December 1968) and "The First and Last of the Yiddish Theater," by Harold Clurman (February 1974).

Ida Nudel's autobiography, *A Hand in the Darkness* (New York: Warner Books, 1990), is a detailed and dramatic account of her life in the Soviet Union. It was also helpful to review newsletters published by various advocacy groups as well as newspaper accounts of her struggle, release, and arrival in Israel. I am grateful to Ida Nudel for reviewing the chapter that I wrote about her. A personal meeting with her provided additional details and nuances.

I am also grateful to Shoshana Cardin for sharing with me the details of her private meetings with George Bush and Mikhail Gorbachev. Most of the material for this chapter comes from a personal interview conducted in June 1993. I was also fortunate to meet with Malcolm Hoenlein and Martin Wenick, who played important roles in the events described. I am grateful to Shoshana Cardin for reviewing the text and correcting important details.

Many thanks go to Yael Arad who took time from her training schedule to talk with me about her life in judo, particularly the road to Barcelona and her silver medal. The press was of course full of articles about her Olympic debut and Israel's first Olympic success. I am also grateful to her for reviewing the chapter.

Nehama Leibowitz declined to be interviewed for this book. In fact, she would have preferred that I not write about her at all. But not including her would have meant omitting the woman who has made the greatest contribution to the study of Torah. I am indebted to her friends, colleagues, and former students who were willing to talk with me about her methods and her impact. They include Marla Frankel, Edward Greenstein, Ben Hollander, Walter Hertzberg, Avraham Holtz, Shlomo Riskin, Uriel Simon, and Moshe Sokolow. Articles by Zev Harvey, Aryeh Newman, and Rachel Salomon also provided insights. I of course take full responsibility for the chapter, and I sincerely hope that it will bring no displeasure to Nehama Leibowitz herself.

The photographs for this book have been gathered from a variety of sources. Jane Shalom, of the *Jerusalem Post* Photo Archive, graciously opened her files to me and provided velox prints of a number of photographs. The Central Zionist Archive in Jerusalem was a marvelous source for photographs of Henrietta Szold and Youth Aliyah. The Yad Vashem Photo Archive provided beautiful photographs of Zivia Lubetkin and other women of the Warsaw ghetto. Erika Gottfried, of the Tamiment Institute Library at New York University, located appropriate photographs for the chapter on Rose Schneiderman. Yael Arad, Shoshana Cardin, and Ida Nudel graciously provided photographs from their personal collections. Many thanks also go to Sarah Feldman, of Behrman House, for obtaining additional photographs and for her careful work in overseeing the publication of this book.

My husband, Daniel Segal, and our sons, Eli and Josh, offered encouragement and advice at every stage of the project. The following people also read and commented on versions of the manuscript: Sara Coen, Jonathan Diamond, Rela Geffen, Grace Goldin, and Philip Warmflash. I am grateful for their suggestions, and I of course take full responsibility for any errors in the final product. It gives me special pleasure that Grace Goldin, a gifted poet and writer, was able to enjoy these chapters before her death last summer. Her creativity and passion for her work have been a source of inspiration to women of all ages.

Sheila Segal
June 1996

Index